Religion

History and Mystery

~~~

By Steve Copland

Religion: History and Mystery

Published by Steve Copland at Smashwords

Copyright 2011 by Steve Copland

All rights reserved solely by the author.

The author guarantees all contents are original and do not infringe upon the legal rights of any other person or work. No part of this book may be reproduced in any form without the permission of the author.

Credits
Cover design by Nikolay Apostle
Proofreading by Cindy R

Contents

Introduction

Chapters

1. Antediluvian World   6
2. Sumerians, Babylonians   15
3. Zoroastrian Tradition   25
4. Hinduism   31
5. Buddhism   46
6. The Americas   55
7. China and The East   66
8. Egyptians   75
9. Judaism   82
10. Greeks   94
11. Romans   101
12. Christianity   108
13. Islam   121
14. Gnosticism, Kabbalism   132
15. Mormonism   139
16. Baha'i Faith   145
17. Jehovah's Witnesses   155
18. Atheism   162
19. New Age Religions   174
20. Conclusions   185

Introduction

Religion. When you hear this word, what comes to mind?

War, power, greed, brainwashing? Maybe other words which have their place in history: inquisition, witch-hunting, burning, torture? Or words we hear in our own history: jihad, extremist, suicide bomber? And there are other words spoken by dreamy-eyed gurus: peace, love, unity, consciousness, or words from those who consider themselves above religion: science, evidence, delusion, superstition, myths and fairytales. Religious history is full of such words.

It was only about 150 years ago that the world believed religion would die, but since then millions have died because of religion and thousands continue to die in religious wars. Today you can't walk back to your barracks on a quiet London street, climb a mountain in Pakistan, or run a marathon in Boston without wondering if some crazy fanatic will mutilate or blow you to pieces defending his perverted version of 'God'. The war against terrorism is a war against religion, a war that may never end. What drives such people to put aside mercy, to be filled with hatred for those who refuse to submit to *their* god or goddess?

And those who tried to wipe out religion have done no better towards their fellow men. Scientific atheism murdered around 120 million people in the last century, and still religion survived. For thousands of years wars have been fought on behalf of the gods whom people served. History is a bloody trail of hatred and intolerance, conquest and slavery, raping and pillaging. Will it never end?

If the history has any chance of making sense, the answer may lie in mystery, in the unseen forces which drive people to forms of religious insanity. The world is full of mysteries, stories, myths, legends and folk-lore, most with enough evidential truth to warrant investigation - lost cities which sunk beneath the waves, a Great Flood which changed the continents and climates of the world, huge creatures whose skeletal remains adorn our museums, footprints of giants embedded in stone, and stories of gods who rode great chariots and ruled powerful civilizations.

Why are these stories found in every ancient culture, in every civilization? The supernatural works of sorcerers, enchanters and magicians; the dreadful power of shamans and priests who claim that creatures from another dimension enter and control them; the hunger for blood and sacrifice; the altars and circles of stone where thousands were offered to appease beings whose origins are not of this world? Is there an unseen war which is played out in the world that is seen? Are those who are driven to madness driven by powers who seek to destroy any possibility for peace? Is there one common root of evil which manifests itself in religion, a force of evil which marches under the banner of death, a bloodstained flag which has been carried by those who have been deceived and seduced by their own desire for power?

The mysteries of religion reveal common threads which may open our eyes to understanding our bloody and evil history. Perhaps we can find an answer to why a man can nurse his child on his knees, laughing and loving before he tucks her into bed, and then rise, have breakfast, and go to the camps where he shoves another's naked child into a gas chamber, shutting his ears to the screams beyond the steel doors. A human life may be regarded as the most precious thing and yet be discarded in a passion of hatred so vile as to wipe away any trace of its existence.

In this book we will take a walk through history, examining the religions of both ancient and modern people in separate chapters. We will ask questions of each in turn, seek the common threads which bind them together, reveal the contradictions, and seek to uncover the mysteries which hold the keys to understanding who we humans really are.

Chapter One: Antediluvian World

Throughout the ancient cultures of the world there are approximately 250 stories, myths and legends about a great deluge, a flood which destroyed all or part of the early civilizations of the world. There is also a great deal of scientific evidence to suggest that such an event occurred. Fossils which have been found in terrestrial deposits are often those of birds and animals which have been trapped in huge mudslides, their bodies whole and preserved. Science calls the evidence of the flood 'catastrophism'.

The majority of geologists agree that at some point in our ancient past the land masses we now have were split away from perhaps one huge continent. Creation scientists believe that this happened at the time of The Great Flood. In this chapter we will examine the writings of ancient peoples who told stories of this time in human history, who spoke of The Flood and the earth being torn apart, of great islands that sunk beneath the waves and others which were born of volcanoes. It is in this context that we can attempt to understand the beginnings of organized religious practices.

Origins of Civilization

In the 21st Century there are two common explanations given for the origin of human life. Macro-evolution theorizes that life began without the intervention of any god or plan. The 'big bang' theory suggests that our universe came into being quite by accident; however, a fundamental law of nature insists that where there is an effect there must also be a cause. Stephen Hawking, the English professor who first postulated the big bang theory, admits that his theory is really impossible without a catalyst, something or someone to begin the process. However, Hawking, who is himself an atheist, has put forward another theory in order to try and nullify the obvious conclusions of the big bang theory and do away with the need for God as the 'first cause'.

He suggests that the universe was a great black hole in which there was no time, and from this came the seed of the universe. His conclusion is that God cannot exist because there was no time before the big bang for Him to exist within. Most Christian theologians would laugh at such a hypothesis. According to the Bible, God has made it very clear that He was the one to invent time; in His essence He exists outside of it. One may also argue that if nothing can exist outside of time, as Hawking suggests, then neither can his black hole exist either. The problem of God as the first cause of the universe hasn't gone away, despite the best efforts of those we consider intelligent.

Apart from that particular problem is the fact that since the invention of extremely high powered microscopes and other data-collecting technologies, scientists in various fields have been confronted with the most intricate and complicated evidence for Intelligent Design in even the most simplistic of life forms.

The single cell is a case in point. Once thought to be a simple thing, it is now marveled at, for it is more complex than about 150,000 computers all linked together, indeed, more complex than anything yet designed by humanity. Cells are the building blocks of life; they need proteins to come into being, and those particular proteins can only be manufactured by cells themselves. This raises the obvious question of where the first cell came from.

Those who reject the proposition of an Intelligent Designer are silent on this question, except for those who turn to the idea of alien beings seeding our planet - a desperate solution, for the aliens themselves would have to have been designed, or be the intelligent designers which macro-evolutionists reject. In this book we are not going to spend a lot of time debating evolution versus intelligent design, but rather study what ancient peoples themselves believed.

The Hebrew Bible records the story of God creating the universe and the earth. In the first two verses of Genesis, the first book of the Bible, an explanation is given and an order of creation which is remarkably similar to our modern understanding of the formation and expansion of the universe in which we live. The Bible tells us that God created humanity in His image and likeness. What does that mean? Basically, that human beings are different to all other creatures on the planet for several reasons, including the fact that we are self aware. Humans use words like 'me' and 'I'. We know that we exist; we recognize ourselves as creatures, whereas, as far as we can tell, all other creatures simply act out of instinct and are not aware of themselves as creatures.

Within several other cultures, such as Chinese and Sumerian, there are similar creation stories of humans being created by one God and placed in a beautiful garden. The Babylonian text, *Enûma Elišh* is quite similar to the biblical account. The first humans were mostly monotheistic, they believed in one God. His name was Elohim, but to the Sumerians who wrote of Him He was simply El. The stories differ in the details, and it is difficult to distinguish between myth, legend and fact. Keep in mind that if there was anything written or recorded before The Flood, these records have been lost to us; therefore, all of the stories we have were handed down orally from generation to generation until they were eventually recorded.

The oldest writings found date back to about 2600-2000BC. There are other forms which are older, but these are simple glyphs or depictions, and it is debated if they are a real written language at all. Some ancient civilizations used carved pictures in a sequence to tell a story, but of course such pictures can be read to mean any number of things and, therefore, may only be useful for the people who created and recorded them. Pictures of men wielding spears and other weapons may tell the tale of a war, but which war?

Alphabets and readable writing occurred with the invention of cuneiform and is best known in the Sumerian, Akkadian, and Egyptian peoples of the Bronze Age. One of, if not the oldest piece of religious writing, dates back to about 2000BC. It is written about the last Sumerian king who lived before the Great Flood and contains laws and advice on living morally, quite like the Bible's book of Proverbs. In another Sumerian text, *The Kesh Temple Hymn*, there is an account of a god and goddess creating human beings, a similar text to *Atra-Hasis*, an Akkadian epic.

One common theme throughout much of ancient literature is that of giants ruling the world before the Great Flood. Many texts record creatures called by various names, including the 'Watchers'. The Watchers are said to be angels, creatures who witnessed the creation of humanity from their place in the cosmos or 'heavens'. These angels/gods were all male and incapable of producing children of their own. About 250 of them, according to the *Book of Enoch* chapters 7-20, changed their form to flesh and blood and seduced or took human women and produced various races of giants known as the Nephilim and Elioud. The names of twenty of the Watchers are given, and also that they were of different heights.

In the *Pyramid Texts* of the Egyptians, the Pharaoh believes that the Watchers will meet him on his afterlife journey. In the Bible (Genesis 6) the Watchers are referred to as the 'Sons of God', angels who fell from grace because they left their created forms and co-habited with human women. The Nephilim were mighty creatures. The *Epic of Gilgamesh* speaks of men living after the Flood who were sometimes 5-10 times stronger than normal human beings and were said to range in height from 3-7 meters. In the *Book of Enoch,* the Nephilim bred with each other and, like humans of that era, lived for hundreds of years.

The Nephilim were soon ruling the world and demanding worship of themselves, demanding people bring them vast amounts of food, and fighting for dominance among themselves. Plato's account of the giants of Atlantis also mentions these wars. They are said to have slaughtered the great beasts of the earth, a reference to creatures far bigger than domestic animals, such as cows and sheep, and possibly to dinosaurs. Enoch gives very precise details of what they did to humanity. In chapter 8 he writes:

> Moreover (1) Azazyel taught men to make swords, knives, shields, breastplates, the fabrication of mirrors, and the workmanship of bracelets and ornaments, the use of paint, the beautifying of the eyebrows, the use of stones of every valuable and select kind, and all sorts of dyes, so that the world became altered; (2) Impiety increased; fornication multiplied; and they transgressed and corrupted all their ways; (3) Amazarak taught all the sorcerers, and dividers of roots; (4) Armers taught the solution of sorcery; (5) Barkayal taught the observers of the stars, astrologers; (6) Akibeel taught signs; (7) Tamiel taught astronomy; (8) And Asaradel taught the motion of the moon; (9) And men, being destroyed, cried out; and their voice reached to heaven.

Enoch goes on to say that "Azazyel has done, how he has taught every species of iniquity upon earth, and has disclosed to the world all the secret things which are done in the heavens".

The idea that Enoch expresses is that these angels instructed their children about knowledge that was known only to them, secrets which were known in the cosmos. The result of the Nephilim influence was war, rape, violence, bloodshed and eventually human sacrifice and cannibalism. The Nephilim taught sorcery and supernatural powers, forms of magic which can only be performed by creatures who are outside of the natural world. Enoch tells us that God decided to destroy the world, and the Hebrew Bible tells us that God chose Noah to build a huge boat.

In chapter 5 of the *Epic of Gilgamesh* we learn of another boat that was built. Gilgamesh was also a giant, but according to the previous chapters, there were giants much greater than he who wanted him and his brother dead. Gilgamesh was told in a vision by his own god, that the great God or Goddess was going to destroy the world in a flood. He was told to build a boat.

The instructions are in the text. He hired a great amount of people to help him, and a large group got on board when the rains came. He speaks of water coming from the skies and up from the ground to destroy everything. Later in the chapter he describes how his boat stopped on a mountain. There is a poem in the text that describes how angry El is when he discovers that Gilgamesh and his people have survived. They were all supposed to die.

The story of Gilgamesh is very similar to the Hebrew Bible's story of the Flood, but also different in many ways. Yet, perhaps it answers a lot of questions. If a group of giants survived the Flood, it would explain many things. The Akkadian king, Naram-Sin, who ruled in the area of Babylon (Iran), is pictured in a battle (Stele of Naram-Sin) as at least twice as tall as his opponents.

There are also stories from after the Flood of ancient tribes north of Turkey who were giants, cannibals and terrible warriors. People built high walled cities to protect themselves from these tribes.

Apart from all of these strange stories are those forms of worship connected to astrology. The ancient god Mitra, or Mithra (also Mithras) is represented as slaying a bull in Roman Mithraism. This event was thought to move history from the Age of Taurus to the next age.

Mithra is spoken of in many ancient texts we will examine. In later religious history he is associated with worship of the 'unconquered sun'. In one depiction he is the ancient serpent who has bound humanity, such as described in the Bible. He has the wings of an angel and is surrounded by the signs of the zodiac. He is the king of the Watchers, the gods and the Nephilim.

The Watchers demanded the worship of this being, the most powerful of the Watchers, the arch-angel and Lord of the Cosmos who, in Judeao/Christian tradition, is called the Devil, Lucifer or Satan.

It would seem from all of these writings and more, that before the Great Flood human beings were bred with angelic creatures that ruled and were worshipped. They are written about by the Greeks and Romans and lived in various areas of the world after the Flood also. These writings may raise as many questions as they answer; however, their similarities cannot be simply ignored as superstitious nonsense.

As we shall see, these people were not 'cave men' talking about imaginary sky beings, but rather describing living creatures that walked upon the world.

For further reading:
Reading the Old Testament: An Introduction, Lawrence Boadt, (Paulist Press, New York, 1984)
Bible, Genesis Chapter 6,9,11

Available for downloading on public websites.
The Book of Enoch
The Epic of Gilgamesh
Pyramid Texts
Enûma Elish

Interesting YouTube videos.
http://www.youtube.com/watch?v=dRuxw-nZoJw
http://www.youtube.com/watch?v=omm8Ey8vwbg

Chapter Two: Sumerians, Babylonians

In this chapter we will examine the religion of the Semitic-speaking people who lived in the Near East lands which are now Iran, Iraq, Lebanon, Israel and their neighbors.

We do not know exactly when the Flood occurred, but it was most likely about 6000 - 4500 yrs BC, although some place it as early as 2600BC. The Hebrew Bible says that Noah was a God-fearing man, but the same is not said of his sons. One of his sons, Ham, was the ancestor of the nations which are later, once again involved with the Nephilim (Numbers 13). In Genesis 9 there is a strange story of Noah getting drunk and Ham going into his tent to look at him. There is a strong connotation that Ham was looking at his father with lustful intent. Noah curses Ham for his intentions and his descendents become the religious enemies of the Jews. It is Ham's descendents who later moved south into what is now Israel and founded the homosexual cities of Sodom and Gomorrah.

The people from whom the *Epic of Gilgamesh* came were all, according to the Hebrew Bible, descendents of Ham. Their history is that of the Sumerian/Akkadian and Babylonian people who, it is believed, settled in Mesopotamia, the area which includes the Euphrates and Tigris river basin, around 4500-3500BC. From this group we have the Assyrian, Babylonian and Persian Empires, all warlike people who display incredibly similar characteristics to the people before the Flood.

The Hebrew Bible says that people began to spread out and that all spoke the same language. One of Ham's sons, Cush, had a son called Nimrod. He was a 'mighty warrior' who led his tribe east and decided to build a great city on a wide plain beside the river Euphrates, the city of Babylon. This city was situated in what is now modern day Iraq, about 85 kilometers south of Baghdad. This was around 2000BC. Nimrod's intentions were to stop his large tribe from being scattered and to build a walled city and great tower to use for astrology. Perhaps Nimrod's intentions were to make Babylon the center of Nephilim worship again. God intervened in the process and confused their languages.

Lawrence Boadt in his *Reading the Old Testament,* tells us that Near East ethnic groups at this time were connected by different languages, the two main ones being Semitic and Indo-European in the Near and Middle East. Through the study of languages we can get a fairly good indication of the movements of various civilizations. By this time the Egyptian civilization was well founded by one of Ham's sons, Mizraim, and had been growing for over 2000 years, but was quite isolated because of the deserts which surrounded the rich Nile Valley. We will study Egyptian religion in a separate chapter.

Sumerian/Babylonian Religion

The descendents of Ham were polytheistic, as we would expect from a man who rejected his father's beliefs. The Sumerian's gods numbered around 2000. Some of them were associated with rivers, trees, the weather, etc., much like the people who lived in the same area before the Flood.

The most powerful god of these people was called Anu. Anu was the god of the cosmos, the one who controlled the demons, monsters, goddesses and people. Anu was believed to have taken a wife called Ki and produced a child who became the most important god, the one spoken of mostly in their literature. His name was Enlil. This powerful god was believed to have raped a goddess and produced a child called Ninlil. In the stories of the Sumerian gods there are many similarities to what we know of life before the Flood. Violence and war, rape and seduction are the actions of their gods.

The Sumerians, like the Babylonians after them, considered their gods to be human in form, although much larger than normal, and to have supernatural powers, such as the sun god pictured on the next page.

They claimed that their gods walked among them, coming and going as they pleased. They also have a great deal to say about demons, which are often portrayed as part human and part animal or bird. These mythical winged creatures could be both large and small, and are even said to live in the houses and temples where worshippers fed and served them.

Demons always tried to drive people to evil behavior, and it was also believed that these demons simply served the greater gods.

Sumerian and Babylonian cultures had what we might consider a glaring contradiction. On the one hand they had some of the first written moral codes and laws, not unlike the Bible's commandments of the Old Testament. On the other hand, the practices of the temples and ziggurats (large flat-topped pyramids) were shocking, at least to modern minds. Sacred prostitutes served Inanna, a goddess who was a contradiction in herself. She was the goddess of war, of female fertility, and sexual love.

The Sumerians built temples and ziggurats for the purpose of worship and sacrifice, as in the one pictured below in which the outer walls have been rebuilt.

The temples served various gods and goddess. In most cases the ziggurat stood in the center of the city and was dedicated to a particular god. The priests were considered mediators and mediums between the people and the deity and had the power of life and death over the people. When disaster struck, such as famines, floods, wars or disease, the priests demanded sacrifices to appease the angry gods. When enemies were captured in war, often the entire population of survivors was taken as slaves and eventually all sacrificed as offerings for the victory. In their art, sometimes a giant is seen depicted as standing beside the priests when these sacrifices occurred. It also became common for people to offer their firstborn child as a sacrifice to ensure future children.

Ziggurats were multifunctional. On the flat top surface sacrifices were made, and in the rooms underneath, temples to various goddesses provided worshippers the opportunity to serve the goddess of fertility in sexual practices. Smaller temples were dotted around the cities for people to offer grain, flowers and food to less powerful gods, but the entire culture was dominated by the idea that the gods must be served, kept happy and satisfied, or the consequences would be terrible. The gods are often depicted as humans with wings in the same way as the Watchers were said to appear.

The practice of sorcery, magic, astrology and channeling spirits was an everyday thing. Priests were chosen for their ability to perform supernatural acts, such as producing fire from their hands and healing diseases. Priests had the power to bless or curse, and the curse of a priest could bring instant and excruciating death to the victim. Priests were feared because of the power they wielded, but the priests were subject to those gods which roamed from city to city, creatures of greater stature than the majority of people.

The Babylonian Empire followed the Sumerian and included the god Marduk. Babylonian religion was very similar to Sumerian, but Marduk was the chief god of the Babylonians. Marduk was believed to have gone to battle against the goddess of chaos and, after defeating her, put the cosmos into order and created human beings. His exploits are told in the epic *Enûma Elish*.

Canaanite Religion

Most Near Eastern cultures had similar religious practices to the Sumerians and Babylonians, but a change begins to occur with the development of the Amorites and Canaanite people who included the 'Sons of Anak', a Nephilim. The Amorites and Anakites were said to be ruled by giants, and many of them were considered twice as high as normal people. They are closely related to the Canaanites, all being descendents of Ham.

In the Book of Numbers (Bible), chapter 13, we read about the Jews coming to the land of Canaan and finding the Nephilim there. This is the land that God gave to Abraham about 500 years earlier. Abraham went to live there, taking his nephew Lot with him. There is no mention of giants in the land, although it seems that Abraham kept to one particular area, the hill country, whilst his nephew went to live near the Dead Sea close to the immoral cities of Sodom and Gomorrah. The Hebrew Bible records that the Canaanites were already living there and, from the description of the cities, were well established.

Canaanite religion is almost a mirror image of the pre-flood era. In the Valley of Hinnon, near modern day Jerusalem, was a statue of the god Molech. This god was depicted as a man with a bull's head and associated with the astrological sign of Taurus and the worship of Mithra. This valley was a terrible place, a place Jesus later used as an analogy of hell, the final destiny of those who reject His gospel. The god Molech demanded child sacrifice, and in this valley thousands of children were burned alive. Leviticus 18:21 mentions this practice and the name of the god, forbidding the Israelites to be involved in the worship of Molech.

Aside from the obvious horrors of child sacrifice were the cities of Sodom and Gomorrah. These cities were the homosexual centers of the world at this time, and dedicated to sex gods and goddesses. These two religious practices lived side by side, one in the valley and the other on the plains near the Dead Sea. Pre-flood religion was predominant here, as in a few other places in the world - a religion of extreme immorality and violence controlled by the Nephilim and their offspring.

Molech was believed to be the Lord of the Raphaim, a line of giant creatures who have only human women in their ancestry. The Raphaim were thought to be exactly as the original Nephilim, the offspring of fallen angels and human women. In the books of Joshua and Deuteronomy, the giant king Og, who was defeated by an Israelite army under Moses' command, was said to be the last surviving descendent of these original hybrids. Og's bed was made of iron and about 4.5 meters long. The Israelites kept the bed in Jerusalem as a reminder of the victory.

The worship of Molech spread to the Phoenician people and into Egypt and North Africa. When the Romans conquered the city of Carthage in 149BC and destroyed the city, they discovered a statue of Molech which was used daily for child sacrifice. According to Roman historians, when the residents of Carthage realized that the Romans were going to defeat them, they believed that the gods were displeased with them for sacrificing low-born children. Therefore, they sacrificed 200 noble children to Molech along with 300 others.

The Canaanite god Baal is also closely associated with Molech. Baal is connected to the bull, a symbol of strength and fertility. Baal worship could be associated with the weather, agriculture, breeding animals and anything connected to fertility, but was also a predominately sexual religion connected to Sodom and Gomorrah and the bull-headed Molech.

The religions of the near and Middle East for thousands of years after the Flood are all very similar. In many ways they resemble the practices which occurred before the Flood, especially within the borders of Canaan, which is now modern day Israel. When God called Abraham and took him to Canaan, he said that this particular land would belong to Abraham's descendents for all time.

He also told Abraham two other interesting things. God told him that from Abraham all of the nations of the world would be blessed, a reference to the coming of the Messiah in Jewish tradition. This child was prophesied (Genesis 3) to be the one who would destroy the work of the fallen angel Lucifer, and that Satan's offspring (seed) would be at war with the woman's child, a reference to Christ. God also warned Abraham that his descendents would be slaves in a foreign land for 400 years, a prophesy which was fulfilled after the Jews went into Egypt, and were delivered 400 years later under the guidance of Moses.

Is it just a coincidence that the greatest number of Nephilim creatures and pre-flood religions were concentrated in the land of Canaan? Many biblical scholars believe that the Nephilim who ruled *before* the Flood were Satan's attempt to destroy humanity before the Messiah could be born. That plan ended with the Great Flood. Perhaps Satan brought his offspring and their pre-flood religion into Canaan after the flood to try and destroy the Jewish people from whom the Messiah would come. The *Epic of Gilgamesh* claims that some of the giants survived in their own version of the Ark.

Much of this is mere speculation, but be assured, the evidence for giant creatures living and ruling on this planet is vast and very difficult to dismiss.

For further reading see:

Reading the Old Testament: An Introduction, Lawrence Boadt, (Paulist Press, New York, 1984)

Chapter Three: Zoroastrian Tradition

When trying to prepare a timeline of religious history, scholars find it difficult to place the man called Zoroaster, or Zarathustra as he is also known. Some say he lived around 6500BC and others as late as 650BC. That is a huge difference in time.

One of the ways we can begin to establish an approximate date is by looking at language. We can speculate that the Tower of Babel was being built around 4500 - 4000BC. People moved in all directions. In the last chapter we focused on the people who went south of modern-day Turkey into what is now called Iraq and established the city of Babylon. In this chapter we are concerned with those who went north and northeast into what is now Turkmenistan, Uzbekistan and even southern Russia. This group later migrated south, conquered the area of Iran, and later continued through Afghanistan, Pakistan and India.

Generally speaking, a group of nomadic people known as the Aryans came down from the north around 2000-1800BC. One large group settled in Iran (in fact, the name 'Iran' comes from the term 'land of the Aryans'), and the other group moved through Afghanistan, Pakistan and settled in India. Recently, an entire city has been discovered in Turkmenistan which was founded by the Aryans.

A short documentary on this topic may be viewed at:
http://www.youtube.com/watch?v=g4y2FItJJo4

The religious beliefs of the Aryans became the foundation of Zoroastrianism and Hinduism. Both religions initially had a similar language and rituals. The *Gathas* and *Avestas,* the Scriptures of the Zoroastrian Tradition, and the *Vedas* of the Hindus, both have, among other things, the following in common.

1. Both used an intoxicating drug called *Haoma* (Avestas) or *Soma* (Vedas) which was made from poppies, cannabis and ethedra, and was used to bring visions and speak to the gods.

2. The word for demon is *deva* (Vedas) and *daiva* (Avestas).

3. Both mention large-wheeled chariots which were pulled by double harnessed horses in battle. The name of the chariot in the Vedas is 'Ratha' and literally means 'chariot of the Rapha'. The word Rapha comes from the name of the giant race the Raphaim.

We know that descendents of the Rapha (King Og, Deuteronomy 3:11) lived in Canaan around 1500BC, so it isn't difficult to imagine that some of these mighty warriors with their advanced technology led the Aryans to conquer other people, bringing their religious practices with them. Much of the past is hidden in legends and myths, but these legends were powerful enough to motivate modern minds such as Friedrich Nietzsche who wrote *Thus Spoke Zarathustra* and *Will to Power,* two books which inspired Adolph Hitler to try and build what he thought was a pure Aryan race of people who would rule the world as the Third Reich. The word 'Aryan' also means king or noble.

Another recent discovery in Siberia has found a fragment of bone and a tooth which have different DNA to other humans. These 'humans' have been called the Denisovans. Such discoveries should make us realize that there is a great deal of truth about the ancient past that we simply don't know.

Zoroastrian Religion

There is little known about Zoroaster, but scholars generally agree that the *Gathas* are his compositions. There is little doubt that he was descended from the Aryans who conquered Iran. He taught that the creator was one god called Ahura Mazda, or just Mazda. His name means 'wise Lord'. Ahura Mazda is depicted as a bearded man with large wide wings, standing within a circle.

Sometimes stars are shown above his head, and the circle is thought by scholars to represent the sun. Mazda is the creator of sky, water, earth, plants, animals and fire.

Ahura Mazda was a spiritual being who had a semi-human form with wings. He also had an enemy who was thought to be almost as powerful who was created by him. This being is the prince of demons and known as a 'drugwant' (demon). His name is Angra Mainyu or Ahriman, and in the Gatha hymns simply 'Drug'. It isn't difficult to see similarities to Judeo/Christian teaching of the One God Jehovah who created Lucifer, a powerful angel who through his rebellion became the prince of demons. Some scholars believe that Zoroaster influenced Judaism, but there are just as many who believe that he was influenced away from his Aryan roots through being influenced *by* Judaism. Personally, I think that the latter is most likely, simply because Zoroaster is seen as a prophet who is bringing a new teaching to his people, and of course the oral traditions of the Jews had been handed down all the way back to the Flood.

Zoroaster considered himself to be in a battle where good and evil were trying to claim his soul in the afterlife. The Gathas are hymns or songs for protection from Drug. Drug and his children are able to take different forms, to produce children, and are associated with crawling like snakes. These demon gods infect the minds of men causing them to do evil.

The Avestas have a much wider view of the gods and consider many of them to be both good and evil. The Avestas, like the Vedas of Hinduism, constitute texts for ritual sacrifices which were memorized by the priests born into this service. These rituals most certainly include the religious practices of the Aryans, as the Vedas were not influenced by Zoroaster and yet are very similar. The rituals themselves are spells and charms, forms of ancient magic which were thought to have powerful effects on both the priests and the people.

The gods they sacrificed to were all associated with diverse areas of life and demanded various types of sacrifice. Some were to control the forces of nature, others to give the characteristics of ferocious animals, turning the person into a mighty warrior with superhuman strength. Others were associated with the fertility of humans, plants and animals, and like the Hindu practices of Tantrism and Kundalini Yoga, involved illicit sexual practices. It was thought that the more uninhibited and lustful the practice was, the more the god would bless the person.

Priests drank the drug haoma before performing the rituals and, in trances, spoke of visions. This practice of using forms of cannabis and opium continued right through to the establishment of Islam, 500-600 years after the birth of Jesus Christ. This drug was also used by the common people involved in sacrifices before engaging in sexual rituals.

The Avestan hymns are somewhat contradictory in their content. The Gathas, written by Zoroaster himself, call for moral living and purity which will bring favor and righteousness from worshipping Mazda and rejecting the teachings of the demons. However, the rest of the Avestas are not concerned about morality as much as correct rituals. Some of the most common gods are worshipped, such as Mithra, the Lord of the Cosmos. Mithra is a god of extreme violence and war, a god who, if the worshipper obeys the correct ritual, gives the initiate superhuman powers to destroy human enemies.

Roman soldiers, centuries later, worshipped Mithra in secret cults. They met in underground temples and swore their souls to Mithra in exchange for super powers. Initiates would lie naked on the ground as in shallow graves and a bull was killed in the ceremony. The bull's blood was sprayed over the soldiers and the high priest then went from one initiate to the other as the soldier bound his life to Mithra in an oath. The high priest held a sacred knife above his heart and, as the initiate recited the oath, his body was said to levitate up from the ground and the knife entered his heart.

Whether or not this ritual was part of the Zoroastrian Tradition is not known, but a similar tradition is held by Shiite Muslims on the Day of Ashura, when worshippers cut their heads and bodies with swords and knives during worship and run through the streets covered in blood. The name Ashura can be traced back to the god Ashura of Zoroastrian tradition.

The god Mithra is also spoken of in the Vedas, and it is suggested by some scholars that this may be the source of the tradition that beef is never to be eaten, and cattle, such as cows are sacred animals. The Avestan hymn to Mithra begins with the words that this text was given to Zoroaster by Ahura Mazda, who created Mithra, and includes the following:

> We worship Mithra ... who, overtaking his opponents, overcome by passion together with manly valor, strikes down his opponents with a toss of his head ... who cuts everything up; all at once he mixes together on the ground the bones, hair, brains, and blood of the men who are false to the covenant.

The hymn to the drug Haoma speaks of Haoma as a god who empowers the person through the drinking of the drug. The person is commanded to give reverence to Haoma.

> Haoma is best for the drinker and the best provision for the soul. I call down, O yellow Haoma, your intoxicating power, strength, victoriousness, health, prosperity, growth, force for the entire body, complete knowledge. I call this down so that I may go about among beings autonomously, overcoming hostility and defeating the lie.

In the Haoma hymn, the person who is drinking the drug is inviting the god ('I call down') to enter their body as the drug enters, an invitation to possession. Through being possessed the person hopes to have everything spoken of in the hymn.

From these examples of popular Zoroastrian scripture it would be difficult to consider this a peaceful religion. Both hymns speak of defeating those who 'are false to the covenant', those who hold to 'the lie'. These people believed that the oath/vow they took to Mithra and other gods was sacred. Any who refused to do the same, or who were not dedicated to these gods, should be slaughtered as in the descriptions given. A similar idea is expressed in the Qur'an which calls for death to infidels.

Perhaps Zoroaster was trying to get the people to abandon their worship of demons and the giants who crushed enemies with their fast chariots. The Gathas, which we know he wrote, are almost a complete contradiction to the rest of the Avestas, perhaps a strong reason for believing that he was influenced by Judaism. Zoroaster called for righteous living and was concerned with morality rather than demonic spells, superhuman power, sacrifices and rituals. Nobody knows, but it is thought that after his death the remainder of the Avestas, which call for slaughter and demonic possession, was attributed to him so that the ancient religion of the Aryans could continue.

The overall teachings of the Avestas continues through the centuries. When we study Judaism we will encounter the affects of this religion again through the Persian and Babylonian kings who lived alongside the Israelites and are written of in the Hebrew Scriptures.

For further study see,
World Religions: Western Traditions, Edited by Willard G. Oxtoby. (Oxford University Press, 1996)

Chapter Four: Hinduism

A few hundred years after the Aryans settled in what is now Iran, a large group of them migrated again, moving through Afghanistan into Pakistan and Northern India. This is known as the Indo-Aryan invasion. Living in the land were the people we refer to as the Indus. Very little is known about them except through archaeology, as they left no written records which are translatable.

The Indus Valley Civilization, also known as the Harappan culture, can be traced back to an approximate time from the spread of peoples at the Tower of Babel. Two main sites have been excavated, Mohenjro Daro (Sindh, Pakistan) and Harappa (Punjab, Pakistan). These sites indicate that the Indus had a well-established culture with public baths, drains and granaries. Female figurines suggest female goddess worship associated with fertility.

In what is thought to be a seal, another image portrays a cross-legged male figure with large horns, surrounded by animals. This figure, and other finds depicting cross-legged figures and bulls, strongly suggests knowledge of the worship of Molech.

The veneration and even worship of bulls and cows, which is still a part of Traditional Hindu belief, can be traced back to this period. It is also speculated that this cross-legged figure may be the first instance of evidence leading to the practice of yoga.

Not much is known about the decline of this civilization; however, with the arrival of the Aryans the entire subcontinent soon became Aryanized, and by the time of the Mauryan dynasty in the fourth century B.C, the religion of the whole area was under the philosophical and religious influence of the Vedas.

The Vedas

The Vedas are principally the works of the Aryans, a collection of hymns which are recited, chanted and sung. The Vedas contain four main themes: sacrifice, creation, order, and gods and goddesses. The idea of rebirth doesn't occur in the Vedas; that is a later development in the Upanishads. The Vedas were written by seers and poets, yet they are said to be without human authors, rather, they are the eternal sounds which are found in the heart of every person who desires knowledge of his/her existence. The words of one hymn, (1.164.37) express the desire for this knowledge.

I know not what I am: I wander alone with a troubled mind.
Then comes awareness...

These words portray the desire of every human being to know why we are created and our purpose in life.

Sacrifice

Understanding the Vedas can be a complicated business as they evolve rapidly. Three principal gods are spoken of in the earliest writings, Agni, Vayu and Indra. These three constitute fire, life (wind, breath, lust) and war. The key word in understanding Vedic literature is 'sacrifice'. Sacrifice is at the heart of all Vedic religion. In the beginning, in general terms, sacrifice is made to *appease* the gods, but as the Vedas develop, sacrifice is made to *control* the gods as the elevation of self became the center. The order and ritual of each sacrifice was considered absolutely crucial. If the sacrifice was done incorrectly, the god would either not act at all, or act to punish. Without sacrifice the gods refuse to act. The priests then are the most important and powerful people as they perform these sacrifices.

The priests prepared an altar, often around a fire, and placed empty seats for the gods who were always invited. After this the Soma, the hallucinogenic drug containing poppies (opium) and cannabis (called the sacred grass) was taken by the priests, and the sacrificial rituals began.

The very first hymn of the Vedas is to Agni, the fire god who is depicted with a weapon in his hand. He is the principal god to whom sacrifice must be given. Indeed, he is the accepter of sacrifices. This first hymn has many lines which echo both the pre-flood worship of the Nephilim, and the Hebrew Bible's account of Lucifer. In Isaiah 14 and Ezekiel 28 the Bible refers to Lucifer as a 'chosen guardian cherub', a priestly angel, who 'walked among the fiery stones' until he was cast out of heaven with a great host of fallen angels. His name means 'beautiful or radiant one'. Genesis 6 of the Bible tells us that the children of the fallen angels and humans were great 'heroes', men of renown known for their prowess in battle. See the following lines from hymn one:

> Lord Agni, the chosen priest, god, minister of sacrifice...he shall bring forth the gods...he is rich in heroes...ruler of sacrifices...to thee dispeller of the night, bringing thee reverence we come...radiant one, lawgiver, increasing in thy abode...be easy for us to approach, even as a son to his father.

The second hymn of the Vedas is primarily addressed to Vayu, the god of life. The hymn calls for Vayu and Mithra to come to the worshippers who have prepared the Soma, taken the drug, and are ready for their encounter with these gods. Keep in mind that Soma was an integral part of Vedic worship; therefore, during the sacrifices priests were nearly always experiencing hallucinogenic trips. As one reads the hymns, the priests performing the sacrifices tell of seeing bright, angelic, godlike creatures. It would be too simple to dismiss their experiences as mere hallucinogenic 'trips', for there seems to be a consistent meeting of 'gods', who in return pass on their version of 'truth' and wisdom. The experiences speak of the gods giving power in war, wealth and riches.

The god of war, Indra, is often depicted in the hymns as the giants who led their worshippers in battle, standing in great chariots with superhuman strength to destroy all who oppose them. Here are some of the lines of hymns 6, 7 and 8 to Indra.

> Those who stand near him as he moves feel his power...On his chariot is yoked the two great steeds (horses) he loves, the bearers of the chief...Your followers throw off the state of unborn children and assume sacrificial names...Indra has near to him his two great steeds and chariot...he can see afar, he slays a

thousand enemies with mighty and awful weapons...he is the irresistible ruler who drives the people with his might...he is our god and no others...with his mighty missiles he defeats his enemies...he fills his belly with Soma.

As we read further into the Vedas the names of other gods appear, all of whom are invited to the sacrifices to drink the Soma and be worshipped.

Creation

The first nine books of the Vedas consistently speak about war, wealth, and those experiences associated with conquering enemies, consistent with the Aryan invasion and take-over of the Indu Valley and into India. As we come to the tenth book, we begin to read about wives, children, cattle, agriculture and the developments of gambling houses, etc. Cities were being built or captured and assimilated into Aryan culture and, as the people settled into the land and battles decreased, the writings take on a more philosophical approach as priests are thinking more about life rather than defeating their enemies. Soma still plays a predominant role in sacrifice, but as life changed, so the roles of the gods changed with it.

The date is now around 1000BC, the same time that King David established Jerusalem as Israel/Judah's capital. The Aryans have conquered India and the caste system has been established.

There are five castes. Only the top three were Aryans.

1. Brahmins. Priests who control the sacrifices.
2. Ksatriyas. Warriors.
3. Vaishyas. Merchants.
4. Sudras. Non Aryans. Serfs/slaves from the people who were conquered.
5. Outcasts. People considered untouchables who were subordinate to all.

In the Vedas we begin to encounter the names of many other gods which very often appear as the result of visions and trances during Soma-induced worship. The word 'heaven' appears frequently as the priest's role moves from sacrificing for victory to seeking the gods for answers about life and death. The mention of ships shows us the advancement of trade, not only by land routes, but by sea, and of course with trade and connections with other cultures, the influences of the religious ideas of other people can be traced in the Vedas.

In book 10.121 we read the hymn to the 'Unknown God', also called the Hiranyagarbha Sutra. This hymn can be dated at approximately 1000-800BC.

> In the beginning...Only Lord of all created beings...He put in place the heavens and the earth...the giver of breath...he whose commandments all the gods obey...He is the God of gods and there is none beside him...what God shall we adore with our oblation?

This hymn marks the first time we see the idea of one Lord/God above all others in the Vedas. By this stage in history the first 5-10 books of the Old Testament have been written, practiced and memorized by all Jewish males. Many of the lines from this hymn are exactly as in Genesis, Exodus, Leviticus and Deuteronomy. Is this a coincidence, or did merchants trading with the Jews bring these ideas back to India? Throughout the hymn the same question is asked: 'What God shall we adore with our oblation (sacrifice)'? The hymn goes on to say that this Mighty God watched the great flood waters, and that from this flood came the god Agni, the one who was formerly considered the greatest god of the Aryans, the subject of hymn one.

We can only speculate as to the reason there is this huge shift in belief, but the question 'what God shall we adore' is soon answered in the later writings of the Brahmins. Up to this point the Brahmins are in the position of controlling the gods by the exact ritual of their sacrifices, but the God of the Bible cannot be controlled. It is at exactly this point in Indu/Aryan history that the Brahmins demanded greater power and ordered more expensive sacrifices. Their actions forced some to leave, and the religion of Jainism was born.

But perhaps the most important shift in their thinking was in their refusal to submit to the 'One God' they had either learned of or discovered. They gave Him the name Brahman; they called the human soul Atman, and eventually decided that the two were one and the same. The word Brahmin, the priestly caste, simply means individual, but the word Brahman (with an 'a') became the 'supreme self'. In essence, the teaching that many generalize as Traditional Hinduism was born, the idea that we are Brahman, we are God. The 'One God' was rejected as a Supreme Creator to be worshipped, and self was set up in His place.

One vehicle for reaching godlike status is yoga, a practice most likely connected to the original worship of Molech. Yoga developed into a complex system of practice and belief and has several branches of thought. Traditionally, yoga has eight steps which include self-control, observing cleanliness and prayer, postures, breath control, detachment from the world, concentration, meditation (almost in trance), and trance, the state in which there is no awareness of the world and no accumulation of karma. Yoga is seen as a means of gaining salvation.

In later Kundalini yoga, this practice is associated with extreme sexual practices and goddess worship. The practitioner envisages the body as having a coiled snake which begins in the genitals and moves up through the spine. It is thought that the snake is the goddess Shakti, and when she is released, she ascends from the genitals to the head where the Supreme Being Shiva dwells, they have sex, and the person experiences bliss.

The basic idea is to awaken the snake by indulging in whatever is considered forbidden, such as drunkenness, adultery, fornication, certain foods, etc., and these practices will lead to mystical bliss. These same ideas were prevalent in the lands which the Aryans had previously conquered.

Points to Ponder

It is important for the scholar of Hinduism to understand that, unlike the Bible, which cannot be added to, the sacred writings of Hindus are an open system. This means that at any time more can be added and that new teachings may completely contradict the old. A classic example of this is seen in a contrast between the Vedas, Upanishads, and Puranas. We noted that the early Vedas never speak of one God/creator until the 10th chapter. The Upanishads, generally speaking, teach that humans are God, but the later Paranas, written after the New Testament, speak about several gods who are supposed to be the supreme creators, including Shiva and Paramatma, about various sins, heaven and hell.

What is evident in Hinduism is that whenever other religions influence or challenge its teachings, such as Christian missionaries in the first century, it takes those ideas, adds its own interpretation, and includes them into its new scriptures while often rejecting the main teachings of those religions. This practice makes it almost impossible to know what Hinduism really is, unless of course it is a religion in which one can worship anything from a cow, one's husband, guru, god, goddess, myth or self. All of these are acceptable and expected in Hindu texts and laws, depending on which texts one reads.

Upanishads: The Practice of Hinduism

Understanding the Vedas and Upanishads is a complicated business to say the least. One reason for this is the fact that there are a multitude of interpretations and contradictions, partly because of the way that Indian philosophers tried to build on the knowledge of each generation. This means that within a few generations the entire philosophy may have changed as new ideas and knowledge are added to previous ideas. On top of this are the influences of other cultures outside of India, and disagreement between philosophers within. For the student of Hinduism, where one steps into these developments may determine what one believes Hinduism teaches. Keep in mind that the first Upanishads go back to about 800BC and were still being added to in the Medieval Period, and even up to 1600AD.

During this period, Indian religious thought encounters the philosophy of men like Plato, the Judaic prophecies of the Incarnation of Christ, Christian thought and others, and without a doubt these have had strong influences which are discernible throughout this 2,400 year period. In truth, it would be impossible to clearly state what all Hindus believe, for there may be only a tiny percentage of ideas which all have in common. Therefore, we will look at some of the most commonly held views and attempt to explain them without the complication of lots of Sanskrit words.

Traditionally, Hindu life was categorized into four stages or groups.

1. *Bramacari* (students, but only male). These students studied the Vedas and Upanishads as disciples of a guru. They wore a sacred

thread of six strands to distinguish them from others. They did not work, but begged for their food, and their tenure lasted 25 years.

2. Household (marriage). After 25 years with a guru, many would choose to marry. For women there is a duty to produce a son. Producing sons brings good karma and the possibility of rebirth as a man. The husband stays until the first grandson is born.

3. Forest Dweller. This was considered preparation for the next life and an opportunity to spend one's time on religious meditation. Often the wife accompanied her husband, finding food for him and caring for him generally. Under the Law of Manu, a wife must worship her husband.

4. Holy Man. Both women and men could enter this stage, but a woman's husband must first have died. Holy people shave their heads, have no home, do not wash or wear any clothes, walking about naked and renouncing the world. When they die they are buried rather than cremated.

Brahman and Atman

Two words which we have already mentioned are of absolute importance to Hinduism; *Brahman* and *Atman*. The idea of Brahman has several meanings, depending on who you ask, and in which period you are asking. In the early stages of the Upanishads Brahman seems to be a god, an infinite creator very similar to the Bible's description of Yahweh, Jehovah. However, this description changes radically. In simple terms, Brahman generally means the absolute beginning and end of all there is or will be, both physically and spiritually. Brahman is like a life-force which is in all things, the energy which manifests itself in anything from a human soul, tree or rock. Brahman is also thought by some to be a perfect spiritual essence from which both good and evil can be created.

Atman can be described as the immortal soul/spirit of any living creature. A rock has no Atman, but a tree does. Hindu philosophers concluded that Brahman and Atman are one and the same. For a human being, Brahman is trapped within the body of an individual self, an Atman which is moving towards the perfection of pure and perfect spirit. Atman never changes; it is simply an individual part or piece of Brahman.

It may be easier for Western minds to think of this in the terms that Plato suggested about souls. Plato believed that the ultimate God was the Logos. The Logos was immortal, a word which means 'that which cannot be destroyed'. Plato believed that the human soul was a tiny piece of the Logos, and therefore, that the human soul could never be destroyed; it lived on into eternity.

The question of purpose then becomes important. If the goal of the soul/atman is to realize absolute perfection, then how can this be achieved? Onto the stage came the idea of reincarnation and the cycle of the world, that which in later Buddhism is called the 'Wheel of Life'. Imagine Brahman as a self-manifesting creative intelligence/energy which goes through a cycle. Individual souls are part of the cycle.

The Cycle of the World

There are four stages identified in Hinduism as the cycles of the world. These are called *Yugas*.

1. *Krita or Satya*. This is the state of Brahman in beginning the cycle of manifesting. It is a period of peace and perfection which lasts 1,728,000 years. Yet somehow, evil enters this peace and perfection, and begins to take a hold.
2. *Trita*. In the Trita stage only 75% of goodness remains as evil gains strength. This stage lasts for 1,296,000 years.
3. *Dvapara*. This stage sees evil at about 50%. Selfishness and egoism are on the increase. This stage takes 864,000 years.
4. *Kali*. Kali is the black age. Only 25% of goodness remains, bringing strife, wars, dissention, etc. This stage lasts for another 432,000 years. Presumably, we are in this stage at present.

At the end of these cycles is another cycle of dissolution which brings us all the way around to the beginning again. In total, it takes 314,040,000,000,000 years for the cycle of the world of life to be completed. Once completed, all Atman/energy has returned to Brahman and have 1,728,000 years of perfection and peace (Krita period again) before evil somehow creeps in and the cycle goes through all the stages again.

There are differences of opinion about these huge figures. Some interpret them as the years of the gods and that human years are different. The later Upanishads also teach that at the end of the age, a time we are in now, that Braham sends an avatar (a manifestation of God) on a white horse with a blazing sword to destroy the wicked and start a new creation, an idea very similar to the returning of Christ in the Bible's book of Revelation.

An obvious question which arises from this philosophy is how the infinitely perfect Brahman begins to manifest evil? Unlike the Bible, which states that God created angels with self awareness and the ability to choose, Brahman simply manifests itself. In the Bible, some of the angels, being led by Lucifer, desired to be self-governing and to rebel against their Creator, thus introducing evil. Human beings were also given the gift of free will and chose to disobey; an action the Bible simply calls 'sin'.

Yet, the idea of sin is not present in Hinduism the way that Westerners understand it. Sin, for the Hindu, is based on an absence of knowledge, on ignorance rather than a rebellion against one's Creator. Ignorant action has consequences; it produces bad 'Karma'.

Karma

Most Western minds can comprehend the notion that wrong actions bring wrong consequences. We have sayings such as you 'reap what you sow', a Biblical idea. Karma is a similar notion. Brahman, the gods, and humans are all under the force of karma. The process of karma is up to the individual; there is no sin and, therefore, no judge. One can skip several rebirths by acting 'good', but add rebirths by acting 'bad'. Being born as a human being is a rare chance for 'Moksha', for escape from the endless cycle. Humans make up only about 1% of all living things as insects, animals, etc., all have Atman.

The issue for Hindu philosophers is how to explain the problem of evil. If Brahman is a form of creative energy/intelligence, but not a God in the sense of a Creator/being, then within Brahman must be both good and evil, for both have emanated from this source. If Brahman is both good and evil, then how can a mere human decide how to act, and who can determine what evil is?

This is a complicated question that receives many different complicated and contradictory answers within the Upanishads. Some argued that the entire material world is an illusion, that only Atman is real. However, others argued that if that was the case, then the actions of the body could not affect the soul and produce either good or bad karma. This dilemma is discussed in the story of Arjuna and Krishna in the Bhagavad-Gita.

It is not until the 8th century AD that the Hindu philosopher Shankara used these contradictions to prove his theory of the existence of an infinite, perfect God/Creator, such as is described within the Bible. Without a holy and perfect Creator, he argued, there is no way to measure good or evil.

But the idea of karma has other consequences. Consider the teaching that a person is born into one of the five castes in relation to what he has done in a previous life. No one can move up the caste ladder and go from an untouchable to a slave. Only through death and rebirth can this be achieved. This philosophy has been the reason that there have been very few reformers in Indian history.

From a positive perspective, if one believes in evil, and that evil actions will bring bad karma, then this may be a motivation to try and live a 'good' life; it may offer an explanation for suffering, and explain why some are born beggars and others rich.

From a negative perspective, it generates an acceptance of suffering and, more importantly, an absence of compassion for the poor and destitute. If one sees a beggar on the streets, this person can simply be despised and rejected, for he is receiving his just reward for a previously evil life. Karma also creates a very fatalistic view of life, as there is no chance to move upwards until death, so one must accept their fate. There is also a deep sense of injustice because one cannot recall what evil thing they did in their previous life.

Hindus use yoga, asceticism, extreme forms of self-mutilation, observance of religious rituals and sacrifices, meditation, etc., to try and attain a better rebirth on the cycle of life. Women, generally speaking, must first be reborn as a man before they can complete the cycle.

Later Hindu literature includes Ramayana, which is similar to the Bhagavad-Gita, and the Puranas which date from about 100-1000AD. The concepts of sin and hell can be found in these texts as well as creation myths, laws for castes, etc.

Modern Hinduism

The colonization of India by the British in the 18th century has had an enormous impact on Traditional Hinduism. The caste system, which was absolutely ingrained in Indian society, came under attack as Western ideas of equality, and especially women's rights, were introduced by the British. The British were horrified to see widows throwing themselves onto the funeral pyres of their husbands in the hope that being burned to death would give them a chance of rebirth as a man. Coupled with this was the problem of deforestation, as huge amounts of wood were used to build such fires.

However, the caste system still exists, although in a different form to the original.

1. Brahmans (6%). The highest caste makes up about 6% of the Hindu population. They are considered to be the purest of Orthodox Hindus and wear a 'sacred thread' over their shoulder to signify their superior 'twice-born' status. Brahmans still become priests, but are also well represented in government jobs.
2. Upper Classes (14%). These are the 'forward castes', in official terminology, and, generally speaking, include landowners, factory owners, merchants, doctors, and people in high paying jobs. Some of these have a deserved reputation (Thakurs) for harsh exploitation of low-caste workers.
3. Lower Castes (52%). Those Hindus who are classified as 'backward' by the government. These are principally laborers, farmers, servants, and the rural poor in general - basically the working class.
4. Dalits (18%). Dalit status is so low that they are considered to be without caste. They do the jobs considered most demeaning, such as waste disposal, burning the dead, street cleaning, etc. Upper-class Hindus avoid all physical contact with them, and although the government has outlawed discrimination against them, the majority are still desperately poor.
5. Untouchables (10%). Those born of Dalit and lower caste status who are physically or mentally deficient at birth (crippled, blind, deformed), beggars, and Christians (anyone who has converted to Christianity from Hinduism as this is viewed as a person trying to escape karma).

British influence has seen the rise of many Hindu reformers who have challenged the caste system. India was under British colonial Law from 1772. Prior to this, there are almost no records of legal transactions, and, generally speaking, rulers through various ages set the law through interpretations of Vedic texts. In the major economic centers of India, Traditional Hinduism has become something of a quaint system of holidays and festivals, as the modern generation of young people have adopted international economic values, yet in the small country villages life continues very much as it has for centuries.

The fundamental values of right and wrong have also been markedly influenced by other religions, such as Christianity and Islam. Some Hindus believe in a concept of sin, whilst others do not. India, like most countries undergoing modernization and economic growth, has adopted International Laws.

The exchange of ideas and religious practices went both ways. In the 20th century, Hindu gurus, such as Maharishi Mahesh Yogi (Transcendental Meditation), have introduced their particular versions of Hinduism to the Western world, albeit often packaged in pseudo-scientific forms. When the Beatles decided to learn Transcendental Meditation, millions of their fans followed suit. Within the span of a few decades, meditation and yoga centers sprang up throughout Western cultures.

Points to consider.

The fundamental beliefs of karma and reincarnation cannot avoid having a huge impact on a society such as we observe in the Hindus of India. If we view a person's status of birth as a consequence of his/her actions from a previous life, and forbid that person to move forward or upward in society, then in fact we condemn millions to a life of absolute poverty. Many millions of lower-caste Indians have migrated to the cities in search of jobs, only to be exploited and discriminated against because of their birth status.

On top of this obvious social problem is the issue of the identity of individuals and how they view others. If you are born into a high-caste family, you don't consider this good fortune or feel gratitude, but rather that you are where you deserve to be. A belief in karma gives you an absolute right to hold yourself either in great esteem or in self-hate, depending on your caste. Compassion towards those beneath you is considered a waste of charity, for those born into abject poverty must bear the consequences of whatever evil actions in a past life led them to be born into that status.

If we are here for just one life, as both Christians and atheists believe, then there is the opportunity for people to improve their lot, to show compassion, and not consider themselves better or worse than others simply because of the family into which they were born.

For further reading and watching.

John M. Keller, *The Indian Way: Asian Perspectives* (Macmillan Publishing, 1982)

Some Christians believe that Kundalini Yoga and other forms of Hinduism have demonic origins and that these teachings have infiltrated mainline Christianity. Author Andrew Strom in his book *Kundalini Warning: Are False Spirits Invading the Church?* outlines this view.

Chapter Five: Buddhism

Unlike Hinduism, we can give an accurate date for the beginnings of Buddhism. Siddhartha Gautama, the man commonly referred to as Buddha, was born a prince around 563BC in Nepal. According to tradition, while a boy growing up within the palace walls, his father met his every desire. He married a local girl and had a son called Rahula, but it was not until after all of this that he actually saw the real world beyond his palatial home. One day he took a trip around the city and saw the reality and suffering of the common people. It shocked him to his core. The sight of an old man begging, another sick and crippled, and a dead body being carried by mourners, moved him in such a powerful way that he turned his back on the wealth and title that was his by right, left his wife and son, and began a six-year search.

He was taught to meditate, learned yoga, and mixed with Hindu aesthetics and Jains. Legend has it that he ate the wrong things and was sent away by his gurus. He traveled to Gaya where he sat under a tree until the 'truth' finally hit him. The problem is desire; eliminate desire and one can know freedom. He returned to the gurus, who were impressed by his serenity, and preached his first famous sermon.

Buddhist Texts

The *Tripitaka* are said to be the first sacred writings for Buddhism. The word means 'three baskets', as these were stored in 'pitakis' (baskets). The baskets themselves are divided into subjects, the first being the Discipline Basket with its 277 regulations for monks. The second is called the Discourse Basket which contains the records of the Buddha's teachings and sayings, the basic theology of Buddhism. The third basket contains the Special Teachings, including poems, songs, and stories from the Buddha's previous lives. The Tripitaka are the writings of Theravada Buddhism.

Mahayana Buddhism contains around 2184 sacred writings apart from the Tripitaka. The majority are called Sutras and were developed between 200BC and 200AD after the split from Theravada Buddhism. The main sutra is called the Lotus Sutra and is said to be a sermon by

Buddha about how to become a Bodhisattva, a kind of angel/helper, and how to reach buddha-nature. The Heart sutra is also considered to be very important, as it outlines the ideas of Nirvana and emptiness. The Perfection of Wisdom sutra speaks about Emptiness, a notion which was developed further by an early Buddhist philosopher called Nagarjuna.

Vajrayana Buddhism draws heavily upon all of the texts mentioned above, but in addition uses a number of Tantric texts. Two of these texts have become quite well-known in Western countries, *The Great Stages of Enlightenment* and *The Tibetan Book of the Dead*.

Buddhist Theology

In his first sermon Buddha is said to have outlined what has become the foundation of Traditional Buddhism, namely the *Four Noble Truths*.

1. The Truth of Dukkha. The word 'dukkha' is often translated as 'suffering', but in fact it has a much wider meaning. Dukkha is the empty satisfaction that human beings feel, a desire for more, perhaps even reaching out to perfection. The problem is that everything is subject to change, nothing is permanent. Happiness can be found, but it doesn't last; desires can be met but they return. Buddha's first noble truth is that we must first recognize dukkha.

2. The Origin of Dukkha. The second noble truth is to recognize and understand the origin of Dukkha which Buddha defined as 'craving'. He categorized craving in three ways.

(A). Sense-pleasures such as sexual desires. We sense objects which we believe will provide pleasure, and desire those objects. This becomes compulsive and destroys freedom of action. Desire leads to attachment.

(B). New forms of existence, or clinging to life; the fear of death. Attachment to life brings the desire for offspring, to have physical existence both future and past.

(C). Self-extinction. The desire to die, to be free of this world, free from life. Even desiring to be free of desire can be an attachment, and we cannot achieve freedom until we learn to be unattached.

3. The Elimination of Dukkha. The elimination of craving is the Buddhist idea of Nirvana, one of the most difficult and perhaps contradictory ideas in Buddhism because it refers to the extinction of desire. Western minds might see this as a form of self-annihilation, but there is no self to annihilate in Buddhism. Buddha described this as blowing out a flame, but the question the 'self/individual' asks is, 'where does the flame (I) go?'

4. The Path to the Elimination of Dukkha. This path is known as the *Noble Eightfold Path* which we will study in detail. Primarily, the path is Right Understanding, Right Thought, Right Speech, Right Action, Right Livelihood, Right Effort, Right Mindfulness, and Right Concentration. Buddha's path is not a stage 1, then stage 2 idea, but a whole of life path in which each is dependent on the other.

Before moving on to explore the Eight Noble Truths we need to understand one of the most obvious problems in Buddha's teachings. Buddha insists that there is no God, either in the form of Braham or any other. He also insists that there is no 'self', no real individual. Therefore, several problematic questions arise.

1. Who or what determines the ideas of right understanding, right thought, speech, action, effort, etc.? If it is Buddha who is making this determination, then are we to understand that Buddha is not an individual who has determined these ideas? Where, if not from a man, did these ideas come from? Buddha's answer would be that we are not a 'permanent' self.
2. If there is no individual self, then what is it that is trying to follow the path? In order to follow Buddha's path, a self or something/someone must have a conscious awareness of right and wrong and make personal decisions and efforts to change. Buddha taught that self is not permanent; it's just a step along the way to Nirvana. How can a non-permanent, or any other form of non-existent self, accumulate karma in the first place?
3. If there is no 'God', no intelligent being of infinite wisdom who gave Buddha this path, then again, where did it come from? Also, how can ideas, such as right action, thought and effort, manifest themselves out of anything other than a conscious being, a being aware of the possibility of wrong actions, thoughts and effort?

Buddha never actually offers a satisfactory answer to these questions, which resulted in another form of Buddhism in which there *is* a 'god' or gods known as Bodhisattvas, enlightened/spiritual beings who guide seekers to truth. The only answer Buddha gives is that the problem of Dukkha is found in ignorance, and a wrong view of our personal/essential nature leads us astray. Desire binds us to attachment and endless rebirth cycles. For Buddha, even desiring to do good deeds in order to accumulate good karma is an attachment. The inherent contradictions in this teaching became the subject of a huge amount of what we now call Theravada and Mahayana Buddhism.

The Eightfold Noble Path

From our condition of ignorance come wrong actions, which lead to bad karma, which leads to rebirths, etc. The key is a strict adherence to certain rules. The self, who only exists non-permanently on the 'wheel of life', enters into a strict regime of self-discipline in order to be the catalyst of positive cause and effect.

Buddha gave ten basic precepts. Non-monks must obey the first five, and monks all ten.

1. Do not harm any living thing. This is the reason monks sweep the ground slowly as they walk in order to move insects. However, one may harm a living thing such as a plant in order to survive.
2. Do not steal. Stealing produces bad karma. It could be argued that stealing something from someone would help them to be unattached to it; however, it would then be attached to the thief who desired it.
3. Do not be sexually immoral.
4. Do not use wrong speech.
5. Do not use drugs or drinks which cloud the mind. Buddhists do not use Soma.
6. Do not eat after midday.
7. Do not dance, sing, listen to music or go to the theatre.
8. Do not wear garlands, perfumes, cosmetics or jewelry.
9. Do not have a luxurious bed or one which is above the ground.
10. Do not accept gold or silver.

Cause and effect is very important to Buddhist thinking. Everything that exists only exists because of something before it. If the monk is producing right causes, then the end result will be right effects. Human beings are like a part of a great river in which the individual drops of water make up the river, but even the river must begin and end and change.

For Buddha, there is no single cause to anything. The flame burns because of the oil, but without the oil there is no flame. The flame is therefore reliant on the oil; however, if we believe in gods such as Brahman, we will rely on them, even need them as the flame needs the oil. If you rely on God you'll be dissatisfied, so you must rely only on yourself.

One of Buddha's most famous sayings was; *All composite (permanent) things pass away; therefore, strive for your own salvation with diligence.*

The history and diversity of Buddhism is vast to say the least. Gautama's primary teachings were soon added to by others. Theravada Buddhism tried to keep to Gautama's idea that there is no god, no permanent self, and therefore, salvation is solely up to the individual. This teaching is referred to as the 'first turning of the wheel'. The second main branch of Buddhism, known as the 'second turning of the wheel', is Mahayana Buddhism. The first is considered the broad path and the second the narrow path.

The second type of Buddhism owes its origins partly to King Ashoka, who conquered India in the 3rd century BC. His military tactics were extremely brutal, and after seeing firsthand the bloodshed he had caused in the Battle of Kalinga, where about 100,000 died, he turned to Buddhism. Ashoka eventually ruled almost all of India and made Buddhism the state religion, but a religion which changed quite dramatically from its traditional roots.

Mahayana Buddhism teaches a belief in creatures called 'bodhisattvas'. These are thought to be enlightened beings that are perhaps similar to Western ideas of angels. These bodhisattvas are said to have stored up huge quantities of good karma through their previous earthly lives, and after being joined to a person, can help them find enlightenment.

In the following we can see the main differences between Theravada and Mahayana Buddhism. Compare each corresponding number.

Theravada
1. Psychologically and philosophically realistic. The world is real; suffering is real.
2. Denies any Absolute being behind phenomena or existence. No God, and even no self.
3. Buddha was only a man.
4. Salvation is completely through self-effort. No spiritual beings to help or guide you.
5. Strict interpretation of karma connected to individual action.
6. The goal is Nirvana, the annihilation of Dukkha (suffering, craving, desires).
7. Rationalistic, individualistic, sober. One must become a monk before being enlightened.

Mahayana
1. Psychologically idealistic. Ideas are more important than things. Suffering is not quite real.
2. Most believe in an Absolute being behind phenomena, source of absolute wisdom and truth.
3. Buddha was a projection of the Absolute being and, therefore, a god who can answer prayers.
4. Salvation can be helped by others, bodhisattva/saviors such as Buddha.
5. Karmic merit (stores of good karma) can be transferred to others by spiritual joining.
6. Goal is to become a bodhisattva and help others to find salvation. Nirvana is to become conscious of your salvation.
7. Attitude to life is to be emotionally happy, have concern for others. One doesn't need to become a monk, can marry, etc.

Mahayana and Theravada Buddhism have almost opposite ideas on many topics essential to this religion, yet they do have the following in common.
1. To exist is to have Dukkha, suffering, and salvation is needed.
2. Belief in karma and samsara (action and rebirth).

3. Belief in 'anicca', the idea that nothing is permanent, everything changes and is in a state of flux.
4. Belief in 'anatta', the 'nature of the individual', that no permanent and individual soul or spirit survives death. Bodhisattvas are not, supposedly, 'individuals'.
5. The goal of life is the extinction of suffering.
6. Suffering is annihilated through the elimination of desire which is then a state of enlightenment.

Points to Ponder

The discerning reader can see that within a relatively short time Buddha's teaching had changed dramatically. Perhaps the main reason for this lies in the fact that he never gave his followers an explanation to the most important questions which people ask. Where did we come from? Were we created? Is there a real purpose for life?

Buddha insisted that there is no God, but rather a concept of 'Absolute' which he considered to be neither a real being, nor creator/designer. For Buddha, nothing is permanent; everything continues in a state of flux. Human beings come into existence through cause and effect; they appear in the wheel of life and disappear into the Absolute nothingness as the wheel turns. This Absolute is assumed to be like perfect energy or some such thing, yet without a personality.

This Absolute, then, is nothingness and yet also everythingness; it has no beginning and no end. This is why he insisted that the self as an individual doesn't exist; we are only a part of this Absolute. We think we exist, but it is only a temporary illusion because we are just on this long wheel of life heading towards nothingness, like everything else. The philosopher Hegel taught a similar idea, yet without Buddha's wheel/cycle. For Hegel, intelligence was the Absolute something developing and expressing itself in creation. Hegel thought of the Absolute as a kind of eternal intelligence which was recognizing and developing itself. Hegel's Absolute has a personality, but Buddha's does not.

The problems that these ideas create for people have already been stated, but some are worth repeating as conclusions.

1. Karma is a system which relies on the foundation that there is a difference between good and evil, but if there is no Creator/God who determined right and wrong, then where did such ideas come from? If the Absolute has no personality, then where did ideas such as holiness, right and wrong come from? In the natural world of animals, fish, birds, and insects, creatures simply act on instinct to survive.

We don't call it evil if, for example, a stronger male lion kills a weaker opponent in order to be the head of a pride. This, in evolutionary language, is 'survival of the fittest'. But, as human beings we recognize human actions such as murder, rape, stealing, etc., as wrong - as evil. If a man decides he wants another man's wife and kills him to have her, we call it murder, not 'survival of the fittest'. Why should we change the rules simply because we are human?

The other important question is why we should have any rules at all if there is no God. If the Absolute is nothingness, which becomes something and then returns to nothingness, then why should good actions help this process better than evil ones? Does this 'Absolute' have some kind of moral code? The idea of Karma is ridiculous unless there is a moral standard which is outside of humanity. If the Absolute is not a moral, holy being who has chosen good over evil, then by what do we measure good and evil? And if good and evil do not really exist, then karma doesn't exist either.

2. What is the goal of life? For Buddha the goal of life is to eliminate Dukkha, suffering. This sounds very noble, especially if it is to help the suffering of others. But who are these others? They are expressions of the Absolute nothingness; they only think they exist, for there is no self, no individual in Buddha's teaching. In truth, a non-existent self is helping another non-existent self to alleviate a suffering which is an illusion. Why, if we are not real 'selfs', should we want to help other non-selfs? This teaching gives no solid answers to a person seeking a goal in life. We strive to be good, to accumulate good karma, only to lose our individuality in the 'Great Nothingness'.

3. Dukkha is described by Buddha as a feeling of dissatisfaction; an emptiness within. He concluded that we come into existence from this perfect Absolute and are returning to it again on the wheel of life. This explains our feeling of imperfection. The problem is how the perfect Absolute could suddenly begin manifesting itself imperfectly and why,

if it has been through this entire process (wheel of life) before, would it start over again? Where is the purpose in this? It would seem that the 'Absolute' never learns from its mistakes, never learns to stop accumulating bad karma.

It makes more sense to people that a Higher Being, with absolute perfect morality and holiness, created individuals to experience his/her perfect existence. This being, let's call it 'God', is the standard of perfection. If Buddha had such a God in his religious system, it would explain our goal towards experiencing perfection; it would explain that karma, good or bad actions, are measured against God's moral code of perfection, and it would motivate people to act correctly. It would still need to have a system of freedom to choose, and probably call a willful wrong action 'sin'. However, it would make sense of needing rebirths to achieve perfection and give a real reason for why we feel like individuals and why we feel a pulling power towards perfection.

Without a God/creator/designer, there can be no explanation for morality, no goal to strive for, indeed, no real reason to be here in the first place.

Chapter Six: The Americas

Concrete evidence regarding the nature of early American religious history is still under scholarly interpretation, especially with regards to the Olmec civilization who many believe are the first inhabitants of North and Central America. It was first believed that this civilization was centered exclusively around Mexico, but discoveries of various mounds with sophisticated dimensions, many of which correspond to Babylonian and Egyptian architecture, have forced a rethink. There are few, if any, ziggurats in Africa, but many pyramids. However, pyramids were built as tombs, not as buildings for worship and sacrifice. Furthermore, there is a growing body of evidence that the great ziggurats which have been attributed to the Mayan people may well have been built earlier by the Olmec.

One of the great mysteries of these people is in the giant head sculptures which have been unearthed, three of which are shown below.

Some scholars speculate that the features of these heads are African in appearance and try to find a way to explain how African people may have made their way across the ocean. These heads have been dated from 3500-2000 BC, a time when ocean travel was virtually unheard of. Also, all the seventeen heads which have been found have almost identical facial features which leads to the possibility that these were all made of one person, possibly a ruler or demi/god figure.

Add to this fact the ziggurats of the Mayans and Aztecs, which are incredibly similar to those of the Sumerians and Babylonians as seen in the following examples.

The first is a Sumerian ziggurat and the second Mayan.

The obvious question is why these two civilizations, which were separated by vast oceans, are so similar. Surely this is not a coincidence? One theory would seem to have a lot of credibility. We have already learned of the descendents of Ham who went north as far as what is now Southern Russia. These tribes were ruled by giant beings who worshipped Molech, carried out human sacrifice, and later migrated south into Iran.

Is it possible that a group of these people continued east and crossed the Bering Strait at the time after the Great Flood when ice formed a land bridge in this area, a time thought to be the last ice age? Having crossed, they would have had to travel south to warmer climes to an area devoid of ice in order to find land suitable for sustaining life.

We know the Sumerians and others built great ziggurats to worship their demi/gods. Indeed, according to The Book of Enoch, the knowledge to build such amazing structures came from the Nephilim creatures who ruled them and later died out. Such a theory goes far in explaining both the heads and architecture, not to mention the prolific human sacrifices which were part of the cultures of this area, especially the Maya and Aztecs.

We know very little about the religion of these people, but other archeological finds give us clues. We have noted that in the earliest known sacrificial rituals of Antediluvian peoples and those associated with the sons of Ham after the Great Flood, the Aryans, that the worship of Molech is prevalent.

The cross-legged posture of their priests mimic the statues of Molech which were used for child sacrifice. Other early descriptions of Molech worship show a figure seated with arms extended accepting the sacrifice. The three photographs below are of Olmec archaeological finds. In all three the seated figure appears to be wearing something akin to a crown, and in the last two the hands are extended as in Molech worship.

Numerous articles associated with bloodletting and human sacrifice have been found at Olmec sites, including natural and ceramic stingray spikes and maguey thorns. Added to this is one of the most interesting features of Olmec religion in what scholars have labeled as 'were-jaguar' art. The term comes from the idea that many of the statues found are thought to depict a supernatural being who in Olmec mythology was the offspring of a jaguar and woman. This being was said to have great supernatural powers and in some of the statues, such as the ones below, is accepting a child sacrifice. Added to this are a great number of disarticulated skulls of children and other skeletal parts found at the El Manati site.

Although much of what we know of the Olmec civilization is still shrouded in mystery and speculation, there is no doubt that what has been thus discovered closely resembles ties to the Aryans, Sumerians and other Middle Eastern peoples. No one knows why this culture died out or why they moved from place to place. Did they worship a being who was only part human, did they make great statues of their demi-gods, and did they perform human sacrifices to a god similar to Molech? Perhaps we can learn more about them by the people who lived in the same area after them, the Mayans.

The Mayans

Over the past decade the Mayan civilization has become somewhat romanticized in popular culture. During the last twenty years apocalyptic theories have emerged as many believe the end of the world is nigh. The Mayan calendar was thought by many to predict the end, or at least a new beginning, in 2012. The date has passed and the world is still here; the calendar, which was more likely an invention of the Olmec, will fade into memory like so many other predictions.

The Mayan civilization shares many similarities to other Mesoamerican cultures; indeed, it may well simply be an extension of the Olmec rather than one which replaced the other. Research has shown that the Mayan's writing, calendar and religion did not originate with them, but were handed down and developed. Artifacts that are thought to be strictly Mayan can be dated to as early as 2600BC, a time when the Olmec inhabited the same general area. The calendar itself begins in 3114BC, a time before the Mayan civilization is thought to exist as unique. The earliest known settlements which are identified as Mayan appear in the Soconusco region and are dated around 1800BC.

Mayan Religion

The Mayans developed a writing system not dissimilar to the Egyptians; however, much of their ancient religious history or pre-Columbian history was destroyed by the Spanish Conquistadors who imposed Roman Catholicism upon the people of the area. What can be known is remarkably similar to what we have learned about the Aryan races and their rituals. Like the Aryans, the Mayans' religion is strongly connected to sacrifice, cosmology, astrology and blood. They believed in a supreme god, Itzamna, the creator who is associated with fire - the god who had a wife and created lesser gods. Itzamna was also thought to be the first human priest and was himself created to teach the lesser gods the rituals of blood sacrifice divination, and astrology, ideas which echo the older Book of Enoch.

The Mayans believed that the gods required blood to sustain and empower them. Both bloodletting and human sacrifice were central to their beliefs. Like the Aryans, their priests and shamans were the most powerful people in the hierarchy, for the gods listened only to them. Even their great kings were subject to the power of priests.

Mayans worshipped their gods both above and below ground. Above ground, they built magnificent ziggurats in the center of their cities. The ziggurats served as temples for various offerings and sacrifices. Without human sacrifices, which included opening the chest and ripping the heart out of the victim, the gods refused to communicate with the priests. The Maya were constantly at war with their neighbors, and enemies captured in battle were sacrificed as offerings of gratitude for victory. Ziggurats were often built near large caves where shamans performed rituals to the gods of the underworld. Mayans believed that every departed soul must make a dangerous journey through this underworld; therefore, appeasing the malevolent gods that resided there was essential.

Popular modern culture has sometimes portrayed the early Mayans as a peaceful people who spent their time studying the stars and predicting the future. The truth is much less romantic. Astrology played a large role in divination ceremonies, most of which demanded the blood of the one seeking knowledge of the future, even for something as mundane as deciding on which day to plant crops.

If needing a prediction regarding crops for food, the tongue was often pierced, allowing drops of blood to splatter onto a table. The shaman or priest would then interpret and give advice. For knowledge and success in conception and childbirth, genitals were pierced, or in extreme cases, a child could be sacrificed.

Native Americans

The archeological data and myths of the Native Americans are the subject of ongoing scholarship and controversy. Many scholars agree that the first occupants of North America crossed a land bridge which is now the Bering Strait, but the difference in dates for this can vary by 10,000 plus years. Who were the ancestors of the Olmec people and when did they arrive in North America? Some archeological evidence, such as stone tools and the like, is thought to place nomadic tribes in the area around 10,000 plus BC, however, these dates are extremely variable, and documentation about the tribes which settled is almost exclusively from oral traditions.

In very general terms, Native Americans held a belief in a Great Spirit who was all-knowing, all-powerful and benevolent, and other lesser spirits who were evil. For some tribes there was a definitive dualism; however, this was more closely tied to a form of panentheism, as all of creation was seen as a manifestation of the Spirit rather than a divide between the material and spiritual worlds, often referring to the world as a Mother who provided. Tribes had a deep respect of the material world and strict codes of honor within their societies.

Shamans played a major role in the tribe as mediums between humans and deities, especially within the areas of divining the future and healing the sick. The veneration of ancestors was highly important, as was respecting the wisdom of elders in the tribe.

Several tribes have legends about a flood which the Great Spirit sent to exterminate giants, and stories about tribes of giants who roamed the land, presumably survivors of the flood. These giants were said to be cannibals who hunted Native Americans. The Humboldt Museum contains artifacts related to a tribe of red-haired giants who were wiped out by the Paiute Tribe after being chased into Lovelock Cave.

The Dakota also have legends of a giant they call Haokah who was possessed with supernatural powers. The Shoshone Indians have stories handed down about the Tsawhawbitts who were evil spirits in human form, giants who ravaged their people. According to various old newspaper clippings from the end of the 19th and early 20th century, several discoveries were made of giant skeletons which were around 2.5 meters tall, some having horns protruding from their foreheads. Speculation is rife about many of these stories and hard evidence is scarce.

Points to Ponder

The ancient people of the Americas have much in common with what we know of the Aryans, Sumerians and others, people who were separated by vast distances. The most feasible theory of how the Americas were populated is in a land bridge in what is now the Bering Strait. Establishing definite dates is almost impossible. Many archaeologists use the system of uniformitarianism for dating which presupposes that there has been a constant and uniform decay of natural materials which allows accurate dating.

However, other scientists would argue that the world was a much different place prior to the Flood. If the Earth was surrounded by a canopy of water in the atmosphere, and regions like Siberia had tropical climates, the rate of decay may have been only a fraction of what it is today. There is a large body of evidence for believing in a global catastrophe which changed the climates of the Earth, shifted and separated continents, created the Arctic and Antarctic, and an ice age which receded over the centuries.

We may never know for certain exactly what happened in the ancient past, but we should never be hasty to dismiss the stories, legends, and myths of those who lived in those times, especially when what was handed down by peoples separated by such vast distances is so very similar.

Chapter Seven: China and the East.

Facts concerning the practice of ancient Chinese religions are difficult to substantiate and differ considerably. In ancient China religious practice is nearly always associated with a particular dynasty and ruler, but some of the rulers are thought by academics to be myths and legends rather than real people because of the supernatural actions associated with them. Many academics dismiss anything supernatural as myth or legend; however, if we find the same or similar stories appearing in many cultures which lived far from each other, we should take their stories seriously. Keeping that in mind, we will trace the religious developments in Chinese thought using a consensus of opinion.

Shamanism, is predominant in early Chinese religion, as in most. A shaman is a person who acts as a priest, a mediator between humans and the gods. The shaman performs rituals, sacrifices and reads the results in order to foretell the future. Shamans are thought to be possessed by spirits, both good and bad, or to be like a channel through which spirits/demons/gods speak to the people. Ancient Chinese religion relied on the guidance of shamans who served various rulers through the dynasties. In general terms, the people obeyed the religion of their kings.

Ancient Chinese Gods

The oldest known dynasty in China is the time of the 'Three Sovereigns and Five Emperors', from around 3000-2000BC. The Three Sovereigns were considered god-kings or demigods, physical beings of great stature and size who possessed powerful supernatural abilities. These three taught the people magic, how to cut stone and make fire, and instituted the shamans to serve them. They were said to be sons of the Great God, but born to human women. They divided China's rule between five emperors who served and worshipped them.

Although many scholars consider the Three Sovereigns to be mere legend, mostly because of the supernatural powers and great stature attributed to them, the legend itself raises an important question. If these demigod creatures are mere myths, why do we keep finding the very same legends in so many ancient writings?

We have found these same legends in all of the early writings of the Aryans, the Book of Enoch, Zoroastrians, Bible, Vedas, Babylonians and Sumerians, and will read about them again from the Egyptians, Greeks and Romans. For the scholar of ancient religions, finding stories which are almost identical within cultures and civilizations which were separated by great distances is of utmost importance, as it helps us to compile a form of evidence. Were all of these ancient people imagining things? They do not write about their demigods, great heroes, Nephilim, etc., as invisible spirits, but as great kings and rulers who were physical, real creatures. What is more, a great deal of primitive and sophisticated paintings, carvings, hieroglyphic writings and symbols have been found throughout the East, Asia and Egypt, and even as far from these areas as North and South America, such as in the following two examples.

It would be a very rare coincidence indeed for all of these cultures to claim that these creatures existed, cultures that never associated with each other.

For the Chinese, the Three Sovereigns were servants of a greater god, but because they were different in size and power from mere humans, were worshipped, feared and honored. Later writings speak of banning the sacrifice of children and adult humans, which strongly suggests that this practice was performed during the period of the Three Sovereigns and five original emperors.

Herbert A. Giles, in his work *Religions of Ancient China,* states that:

Fu Hsi, B.C. 2953-2838, was the first Emperor to organize sacrifices to, and worship of, spirits. In this he was followed by the Yellow Emperor, B.C. 2698-2598, who built a temple for the worship of God, in which incense was used, and first sacrificed to the Mountains and Rivers.

The earliest name of a Chinese god is Shangdi. This god is associated with the Xia Dynasty which was founded by Yu the Great around 2000BC. Shangdi is the Great Sky God, or the God who rules the heavens/cosmos. The earliest references to the worship of this god are found in the next Chinese dynasty, the Shang, which takes its name from Shangdi. During the period of the Three Sovereigns, Chinese people believed that these were 'Sons of Heaven', children of the Great God, and this tradition continued through the various dynasties.

Chinese emperors were thought to be Sons of Heaven, divinely appointed by God himself, and for many peasant Chinese people this belief still exists today. The god Shangdi was thought to be too far above mortal humans to be worshipped directly. He represented himself through the shamans and emperors who received worship on his behalf.

By the end of the Shang dynasty around 1045BC, Shangdi has a new name and is worshipped as 'Ti'an' or simply 'Ti". Some scholars consider Shangdi and Ti to be the same god, whilst others believe that Ti, who is represented as a huge man, was created by Shangdi to rule the cosmos under the authority of Shangdi who was too far above all others to be worshipped without a mediator such as a shaman.

The Zhou Dynasty began around 1045BC and is split into provinces, western and eastern. It is during this period that we have the development of the idea of Yin and Yang. The shamans taught that spirits must be honored and served, and that there were both good and evil spirits. Shamans also insisted on the worship of ancestor spirits as well as demons. There is no consistent philosophical teaching among shamanist religions, but fear of demons and angry ancestors is prevalent and predominant right up to modern times. The Chinese believed that an ancestor who was not properly honored would return as a spirit/ghost and persecute the family.

Yin-yang is the concept of interconnected opposites. Fire and water, male and female, hot and cold, wet and dry, darkness and light, etc., represent the opposite sides of different representations of yin-yang. These opposites are not contrary to each other, but each exists to provide existence *to* the other. Modern people often use the idea that good could not exist without evil, a yin-yang concept that one provides a contrast to the other; however, perhaps this is a rather primitive view of good and evil.

Alongside shamanism is the veneration of creation which goes through ancient Chinese religion and found expression in the writings of Lau Tzu or Laozi (same figure), the founder of Taoist or Daoist (same philosophy) ideas.

Taoism (Daoism)

Taoism, or Daoism as it is also known, comes from the word 'Tao' meaning 'the way' or principle. Tao has several meanings in the Tao Te Ching, the book attributed to Laozi, and is rather ambiguous. Tao is said to be ineffable, a word meaning something so profound that it cannot be truly explained or spoken of. Tao is both. Our bodies contain Tao, a life-force, energy which has origins which cannot be spoken of. Taoism has many expressions of worship or practice.

1. Naturalism. Taoism, generally speaking, is the life-force of all living things and the source of that energy. In Western/Christian thought we would understand this as the life-force or spirit of God which animates all living things. A tree is alive because the Spirit of Life dwells in it. This is not the same as speaking of the Holy Spirit who is believed to be a person, one of the indivisible persons of the Triune God. For Taoism, this life-force does, for some, have its origins in a God being, and for others, there is no personal Creator; the Tao is more like a form of creative energy without personality.

Taoism, then, recognizes all living things as linked together. Humans, animals, fish, insects and plant-life are all manifestations of Tao. Tao may be spoken of as the 'spirit' of the tree or animal, a similar concept to 'chi'. Although Taoists writings speak of good and evil, these concepts are linked together in yin-yang philosophy so that neither is thought to be completely good or evil. The Taoist embraces evil, yet also exorcises it on his journey towards enlightenment and immortality.

2. Divination. Tao is thought to have purpose, although this is also quite contradictory in Taoist writings. Taoists believe that the 'spirit' of living things can communicate with human beings. Divination such

as reading runes and bones was common, but also much less subtle forms such as practiced by shamans who invited spirits to enter and communicate with them. The soul/spirit of the dead was thought to be waiting to rejoin the physical world in some form or other, and being non-physical and outside of time, could be consulted about the future.

Alongside this is the practice of exorcism. Those who joined the shamans in their rituals often became possessed by demon/evil spirits and began to manifest all manner of things including frothing at the mouth, rolling eyes, growling noises, self-mutilation and murderous threats. People who began manifesting these things after divination rituals were believed to be possessed. The shaman's job was to call upon more powerful demons, join *with* those demons, and exorcise the evil spirit from the body/mind of the afflicted one.

3. Achieving Immortality. Daoist believed that an individual could achieve immortality through various means including being united with nature, meditation, and keeping the laws of nature in Taoist writings. They also spent a lot of time in pursuit of an elixir of life. This was known as alchemy and is thought of today as the roots of Chinese chemistry. It is out of alchemy that various elements were discovered and products such as gunpowder invented.

Taoism also became the foundation of many of the martial arts. The ideas of force and non-force, defense and attack, can be seen in many aspects of nature such as the animal world. The martial arts were expressions of yin-yang put into external practice rather than internal practice. The internal struggle against evil finds expression and release in practicing martial arts for the Taoist, using breathing techniques and physical forms which are often connected to watching the ways of animals. Many Chinese martial arts are associated with creatures such as tigers, monkeys and even birds such as the white crane.

Confucianism

The philosopher Confucius was born in the 6th century BC. The basis of Confucianism is humanism, that is, that it is entirely possible for human beings to perfect themselves through the observance and practice of moral codes and rules. Confucius denied the existence of

God, teaching that man's highest goal is the perfection of himself, not unlike the later teachings of the father of atheism, Feuerbach.

There are several basic elements to Confucianism.

1. Ren. The notion of Ren is the fundamental idea of 'doing to others as you would have them do to you', or the 'Golden Rule' as it is often referred to. To Confucius, human beings are neither good nor evil at birth, but the actions which they choose to do, or fail to do, determine what kind of person they are. In order to change the actions of a person, education and right practice are required. Ren also has a hierarchical concept. Keeping in mind the absolute power of rulers through various dynasties in China, the emperor's example is extremely important to Confucianism. If the ruler is evil the people will follow his example. The same can be said for parents and older siblings.

2. Rituals. Respecting and observing human traditions and rituals are what make a good society for Confucius. In a thoroughly humanistic society devoid of religion or gods, people are the highest expression of intelligence. Good behavior, following the Golden Rule, and respecting the hierarchy with dignity is the duty of all members of the society. This idea contains a strict observance to loyalty, both to parents and the emperor.

3. Relationships. Relationships, therefore, are to be built on all of the above. Every person has an obligation to live according to the Golden Rule. A man must first be able to govern himself before he can rightly govern others. Concepts such as justice, integrity, morality, propriety, decency, compassion, forgiveness, etc., must be learned and observed, and it is each person's duty to pay close attention to all of these virtues.

Confucianism is very similar to a form of social atheism. Its concepts have been used as a foundation of both democratic systems and even communist ones. Confucianism states that every person instinctively knows the difference between right and wrong action, yet offers no explanation to why that is. Building upon the ideas of yin-yang, it simply takes it as fact that good and evil exist, and that each person must decide which they will choose.

Points to Ponder

Chinese religious practices were later influenced by Buddhism, but changed some of the fundamental ideas in Traditional Buddhism. With the already established ideas of yin-yang, and the teachings of Confucius, Chinese Buddhism accepted the idea that opposites can compliment. Even Dukkha (craving/desires/suffering) has a positive purpose in Chinese Buddhism. Dukkha is no longer viewed as the great enemy to be overcome, but rather embraced and worked through like any other problem.

Chinese religions were extremely varied throughout the dynasties as people followed the dictates of their emperors. However, all of the ideas we have discussed have become mixed together. For example, a person may honor creation and nature, pay their respects to their dead ancestor spirits, (Taoism), try to live a righteous life through obeying the Golden Rule (Confucianism), and seek for immortality through a combination of Buddhist, Taoist and other ideas. Communism in modern China found fertile soil among a people taught to obey their elders and rulers.

The obvious question that is posed by Western thinkers is regarding the origin of life, concepts of right and wrong, good and evil, and creativity and expression. Certainly one can find expressions of creativity and harmony in nature, but what is the source of these things? Also, if one is educated to observe the Golden Rule, then who determines what that rule must be? There is a great deal of virtue in the idea of doing unto others what you would have them do to you, and obviously the world would be a better place if we all observed this, but what is the ultimate goal in this teaching?

If there is no afterlife, and most Chinese believe that there is, then what is the purpose of that afterlife? The spirits of ancestors are easily provoked and will return to bring vengeance on the family who doesn't treat them properly. What does this idea say about the predicament of the dead? Would someone want to gain immortality if the afterlife can be so miserable or governed by the living?

Finally, by what do we determine goodness or perfection in this system? There is no 'perfect being' by which to compare the level of our goodness; therefore, people compare themselves either with someone they perceive as good, or with an imaginary person who has perfect virtue. At the end of the day, this is all very introverted in philosophy but external in practice. The goal doesn't seem to be a reward in the afterlife, but a functioning society.

Chapter Eight: Egyptians

The civilization of the ancient Egyptians has been the focus of much debate, speculation and mystery. The popular movie "Stargate", and later television series, created a lot of public interest in the Egyptian gods. The movie is based on the idea that an ancient alien device which can transport people through a wormhole is discovered. This discovery leads to the uncovering of the mystery of the Egyptian gods, Ra, Anubis, etc., who are alien beings posing as immortal gods, enslaving people on earth and other planets. The pyramids, which in themselves are something of a mystery, are portrayed as alien spacecraft. The history of Egypt is much less mysterious than the movie, but when studied, it isn't difficult to see how the Stargate ideas evolved, for the Egyptian Kings often claimed immortal/divine status.

According to Genesis 10, Mizraim, one of Ham's sons, became the founder of the Egyptian civilization, moving south after the Flood. The name Mizraim means 'two Egypts', a reference to the Upper and Lower Egyptian territories. Further to the South is the land of Kush which is believed to have been established by another of Ham's sons (Cush) who had very dark skin.

An interesting fact about these two sons of Ham is that some of their ancestors are described as far bigger than other people and to be godlike. In our study of other ancient cultures, such as the Aryans, we find a similar thing, and all connected to this son of Noah who was cursed by his father. When we study Judaism we will encounter another of Ham's sons called Canaan, a name associated with the Nephilim tribes who were living in the land named after him.

One of the oldest pieces of Egyptian art is the stone palette from Hierkonopolis which celebrates the victory of King Narmer. This palette portrays a great warrior who is twice the size of his subjects. In part of the scene, the headless bodies of what are supposedly enemies lay on the ground. The decapitation of enemies was a common form of human sacrifice among cultures who claimed to have giant rulers. In the second scene, the giant holds the head of a victim and appears to be about to remove his head. The priests carry long poles with symbols of the gods, leading a procession as part of the ritual sacrifice.

We know from later Egyptian writings that a family from the South conquered all of Egypt around 3000BC and created the first dynasty in the capital of Memphis. The Egyptian name for this conqueror is Narmer, and also Menes.

It is difficult to establish concrete facts about early Egyptians. We do know that the first great tombs were flat-topped rather than pyramids. Some scholars, especially Muslim, believe that these flat-topped ziggurats, and the great pyramids of Gizeh, were built prior to The Flood by demi-god rulers. This however, is unlikely, as The Flood itself is mentioned in the *Pyramid Texts* - writings which were found within the pyramids themselves.

The Gods of Egypt

The Egyptian civilization spans around 3000 years and the names of its gods and goddesses changes depending on time, place and popularity. For example, there are five different gods considered to be the Creator: Ra, Amun, Ptah, Khnum and Aten. Ra and Amun were the most popular of these, the former being the sun god and the latter (Amun) the invisible god who began creation out of chaos. The rising of the sun god Ra was seen as the first sign of order from chaos.

Some of the more important gods were Osiris (male) and Isis (female). According to Egyptian myth, Osiris, who is said to have walked upon the earth, was murdered by his jealous brother Set, a god associated with chaos. After killing him, Set removed his penis and threw it into the river Nile. Osiris' sister and wife, Isis, reclaimed her husband's body, used magic to revive him, and made a golden penis for him so that she could conceive and have a son to succeed him, the falcon-headed man/god Horus.

The god Horus became particularly associated with the Pharaohs. Horus is the warrior god who, when he had grown to adulthood, fought against his uncle Set to avenge his father. Horus is sometimes associated with the sun. Every night he dies (sunset) and every morning resurrects (sunrise). In general terms, early Egyptian gods are put into three categories.

1. Gods of place such as Ptah of Memphis, Khnum of the First Cataract Region, or the crocodile god Sobek of the Faiyum.
2. Cosmic gods such as Nut, goddess of the sky; Geb, the earth-god; Re, the sun-god; and eight different pre-creation deities.

3. Gods associated with various functions or aspects of life. Ma'at, goddess of truth and justice; Bes, god of the household and childbirth; and Sekhmet, goddess of war and disease.

By around 2000BC all of these gods have merged, changed names and been added to. Totems, (poles depicting the gods) show various animals, birds, part human creatures, serpents, etc. Totems were often associated with a phallus and a particular geographical area, and were used as places to center on sacrifice and worship.

The Egyptians were very concerned with life after death, but not in a negative way. Indeed the tomb texts have an overconfident arrogance about them, and even humor. Compared to other nations around them, such as the Hebrews and Babylonians who seemed uncertain of eternal life, Egyptians considered themselves blessed of the gods. Through the divinity of their rulers, even the lowliest slave could be assured of eternal life, even if only as a slave. The Nile provided a rich source of water, and every year when it flooded the fertile land was regenerated. Even peasants who worked on the land considered themselves better off than the traveling nomads who scratched out a living in the deserts which bordered Egypt. The deserts themselves acted as natural barriers against enemy attacks, and the wealth of the country meant that art, leisure, and the development of elite armies were possible.

From earliest times the Egyptian kings believed that through their royal bloodlines they were incarnations of Horus, the falcon-headed god. But later, around 1200BC, this view changed as the view of Horus changed. The Pharaohs thought of themselves as sons of Ra, the great sun god. This is one of the main reasons that we have little or no written codes of law in Egyptian civilization. The Pharaoh was god, the god was here and now, sitting on his throne and his word was absolute, even if it totally contradicted the last king. There was no need for written codes; the Pharaoh was the first and the last word in everything, and his laws were passed down through priests and governors.

Astrologers, magicians and shamans played a large part in advising the king. Although considered a god, the Pharaohs recognized that there were other gods, many of them, and their support was necessary for the prosperity of the nation. It was not until around 1300BC that Egypt began to have problems with her neighbors. The 'Sea People', who were later known as the Philistines, were invading from the Mediterranean and sailing their boats up the Nile. The rich Nile Valley was an attractive prize for such people, and using boats to transport troops meant that moving across the deserts was unnecessary.

However, the Egyptians had perfected mobile warfare in the form of lightweight chariots drawn by a single horse and driven by expert archers. On the plains, these chariots were deadly. From the center hubs of the wheels iron swords of almost a meter in length were extended. The charioteers would drive at speed around an attacking army, creating a great deal of dust and confusion. The opposition was literally cut down as the speeding chariots flew by. The chariots cut the legs off the enemy closest to the outside, while the archers fired arrows and spears into the center.

It was at this time that Egypt had one of its biggest slave populations. The Hebrew people had moved to Egypt and enjoyed peace and protection under the Prime Minister Joseph, but after 400 years and many Pharaohs later, the Hebrews numbered around 2 million. The kings feared that the Sea People may somehow arm the Hebrews, or that the Hebrews may seize the opportunity to rebel from within Egypt. This story we will continue in our study of Judaism.

Points to Ponder

Early in the 20th century, the atheist, Gerald Massey, put forward the idea that there were similarities between the god Horus and Jesus Christ. This became known as the 'Jesus Myth Theory', and was built on the writings of David Strauss. Massey's goal was to discredit the Bible, especially the New Testament, and to establish the idea that Jesus of Nazareth never existed, but was a figure created by 1st century Jews who were tired of waiting for their prophesied Messiah figure. This was not a new idea, but rather a continuation of the so-called Hunt for the Historical Jesus which had started over a century earlier.

Over the decades other authors joined the hunt to discredit Jesus by trying to find parallels between Christianity and ancient religions. Macro Evolution theory was gaining popularity, and any writings which claimed supernatural healings or miracles were seen to be primitive and superstitious nonsense. This form of study has been termed 'parallelomania' and has since been completely discredited by

Egyptologists and reputable scholars of ancient Near East religions. By the late 20th century others had joined the hunt and put forth the idea that Jesus Christ was a real human being who had spent years studying Buddhism and Hinduism in Kashmir, and that His message of enlightenment had been twisted into a Judaistic context.

With the advent of sites such as YouTube, access to these ideas has become available to publishers and viewers alike. The movie *'Zeitgeist'* is a case in point. *Zeitgeist*, like the popular book *The DaVinci Code,* makes incredible claims which have absolutely no evidential foundations but have influenced millions.

Here are some of the claims of *Zeitgeist* which scholars have debunked:

1. *Horus was born on the 25th of December.* In fact, Horus was born in the season of Khoiak, between October and November; however, what is even more important is that the Bible never gives a date for Jesus' birth. The 25th of December was added in the Medieval Period by the Roman Catholic Church to coincide with a pagan festival, hundreds of years after the Bible was written. In Orthodox Christianity, Christmas is celebrated on the 7th of January, another late pagan date.

2. *Horus was born of a virgin.* In Egyptian mythology, Horus is the child of Isis and Osiris. Isis was Osiris' sister and wife, the widow who reclaimed her husband - not a virgin. The myth states that she conceived by making a new penis for her husband, a god who was supposed to have a physical body - nothing like the Bible's claim of conception by the Holy Spirit. Added to this is the fact that Jesus' virgin birth was prophesied by Isaiah (7:14) 750 years before His birth. Copper copies of Isaiah's writings which were discovered in the 20th century (Dead Sea Scrolls collection) have been accurately carbon dated to around 700 BC.

3. *Horus had 12 disciples.* There is absolutely no evidence to support this erroneous claim. According to one Egyptian myth, Horus had four demi-god followers.

4. *Horus was crucified, buried, and resurrected on the third day.* Crucifixion was an invention of the Romans. There is around 2000-2500 years between the myth of Horus and the first person to be crucified. Also, there are no Egyptian myths speaking of Horus being killed in such a way. As has been stated earlier, the later myths of Horus became connected to the sun god Ra who was said to die every evening and come back to life when the sun came up.

The movie *Zeitgeist* makes numerous other ridiculous claims about Christ and Mithra, Christ and the Greek god Dionysus, etc., however, any person who bothers to take a little time to find any truth to these claims will be greatly disappointed. The movie draws on the writings of Dorothy Murdoch (aka Achraya S.) who wrote *The Christ Conspiracy,* a book which sites herself as a reliable source. More importantly, she relies on the writings of the occultist founder of the Theosophical Society, Madame H.P Blavatsky. Blavatsky was a Luciferian, a Satan worshipper who claimed that Lucifer is the true and only god of this planet earth. Both Blavatsky, and the previously mentioned Gerald Massey, wrote for Lucifer Magazine, a publication of Blavatsky.

The Internet provides websites where the Pyramid Texts and translations of Egyptian myths may be read and studied.

Chapter Nine: Judaism

Those who have never studied ancient religions and their writings often have the idea that they are all much the same - full of myths, legends and superstitious ideas. When we read the Vedas and Avestas, both which were written by descendents of the Aryans, we are essentially reading the experiences of priests who were on a 'high' after drinking soma, and writings such as Enûma Elish, The Epic of Gilgamesh, and even the Pyramid Texts are written either as stories or songs to their gods.

The Scriptures of the Hebrews are unique in comparison to the above. They are not simply stories, but history, a history which has been verified through the writings of the nations around them. The man Abraham and the cities he visited are listed by non-Hebrew societies which knew him. The story of the Exodus, when 2 million Jewish slaves left Egypt, is recorded in Egyptian writings as the Pharaoh needed to explain why the previous king lost the most powerful army in the world at the bottom of the Red Sea, an event which allowed the Sea People (Philistines) to invade and conquer parts of Egypt.

Other writings have the visions of their priests and sages; the Bible has the prophets, a group of foretellers unequalled in any other ancient text. Up and until the 1950s, critics of the Bible had proposed that the prophetic books of Isaiah, Daniel, Ezekiel, Micah and others had been written after the events they foretold. For the skeptic there could be no other explanation, as the prophesies are exact and explicit, so much so that, either a God who knew the future had given detailed warnings, or charlatans had written them in retrospect. The discovery of the Dead Sea scrolls closed the mouths of the critics, for copper scrolls carbon dated to 750BC bore the exact same words as later copies of the prophets.

The Bible is more than just the history of a people; it has a supernatural quality which poses questions science and skeptics are unable to ignore or answer.

The Pentateuch

Scholars refer to the first five books of the Bible as the Pentateuch, meaning 'five books'. They are also referred to as the Torah; however Torah, which means 'teaching', can also include the oral tradition which was handed down as the Talmud and Midrash, loosely defined as interpretations and commentaries on the Pentateuch. In Jewish and Christian tradition, these five books were written by Moses under the supervision of God. Jesus also testified that Moses wrote these books.

Creation

Unlike the Vedas and Upanishads, the Bible contains a linear rather than cyclic history. Human history has a beginning; indeed the first book of the Bible, Genesis, means 'beginning'. Genesis opens with a brief account of the creation of the universe, 'In beginning God created the heavens (cosmos) and the earth'. This is a summary statement which is then expanded upon. The opening verses of Genesis begin with the words 'and God said', a statement which theologians define as 'Creation ex-nihilo' that God *spoke* creation into being. Whereas in other ancient literature one or several gods split apart to make land, sky, sea, etc., in the Bible God exists outside of His creation.

Modern cosmology understands that the cosmos did indeed have a beginning. This beginning is called 'Time Zero' and is also known as 'The Big Bang'. This theory is based on the observable fact that the universe is expanding and, therefore, must have originally been as small as the area on the tip of a pin - a tiny seed which contained all of the necessary ingredients for the cosmos.

Scientists can only speculate on where that seed came from and what the catalyst was for the 'big bang' which started the process of expansion; the Bible simply states that 'God spoke'. The next verses of Genesis declare that the earth was 'formless and void'. These words, although not written to give a scientific explanation, can be interpreted in scientific terms as the gases which were present in space - gases which collided, cooled and formed planets, stars and other cosmic bodies.

What is both amazing and thought provoking is that the Genesis account records the same sequence of progress in the formation of planets as our best scientific observations understand our universe to have 'evolved'. Other ancient texts have myths, like the Hindu version of the world sitting on the back of a huge turtle which was standing on an elephant, but the Bible, although written in simple terms, can stand alongside science without contradiction.

Humanity as 'Image and Likeness of God'

The creation of human beings is a highpoint in the early chapters of Genesis. Human beings, unlike all other creatures, are said to be 'made in the image and likeness of God' and given the task of ruling over and looking after the earth. What is meant by 'image and likeness'? The word image denotes a reflection, that humanity alone has been gifted with some of the characteristics of our Creator. The foremost distinction is self-awareness. We, unlike all other creatures, are aware of ourselves as creatures, as individuals. Self-awareness contains the fact of responsibility and choice. Animals and other creatures act out of instinct, whereas humanity has the cognitive ability to make choices based on moral concepts, on conscience, and an awareness that actions have consequences we refer to as right and wrong.

Image and likeness also contains the idea of acting in a similar way. The God of the Bible is creative, not from the point of view of reproducing to survive, but rather an expression of creative love. This is also something unique to humanity. According to the Bible we reflect the creativity of God. Human beings produce children, not out of an overwhelming instinct to survive, but for love, for family, and the desire for intimate relationship. Our creativity also expresses itself through music, poetry, painting, building and inventing.

Genesis also offers an explanation for the *purpose* of creation. Unlike Buddha's wheel of life in which humans appear and disappear into nothingness, the Bible suggests that we are created to be in a relationship with our Creator, in a similar way that we desire to be in relationship with our own children. The goal of creation is that human beings come to know God and experience Him in all His infinite fullness.

Humanity is offered choice. The Biblical story of the Garden of Eden, which is thought by some to be an analogy rather than literal, proposes that part of the image and likeness is the possibility to be autonomous, to make choices as individuals. God has chosen to be 'holy'. The ability to choose must be part of the image of God, for God has chosen to be whom and what He is. Human beings are offered the same choice, for without the possibility to choose, humanity can never know what it means to be autonomous and, therefore, never fully realize what it is like to be like God.

The ability to choose creates the possibility of right or wrong choices. This idea is present within the first few chapters of Genesis - the idea that to knowingly choose what is contrary to our understanding of right and wrong in our god-given conscience is sin. Sin, from a biblical point of view, is not ignorance or even foolishness, but rather a willful rebellion against the holiness and will of God the Creator. In other words, it is when the creature demands to stand apart and rule its own life independent of the One who gave it life, to choose a different path than the path which is promised to lead to God Himself.

Most of the ancient religions we have previously explored seek to find answers to the dilemma of evil in the world. Hinduism offered the stages of the world within a cyclic wheel which turned every 314,000,000,000 years. Buddha's concept of Dukkha led him to seek ways to overcome suffering and craving but couldn't offer an explanation for the origin of that suffering.

The Bible throws the culpability for evil back on humanity's wrong choices - the problem of sin. The first humans chose to rebel and, because of their god-given rule over the earth, their choice affected everything under their authority - the entire world. This is the Bible's explanation for the evil and suffering in the world - an answer unique in that it lays the blame at our own feet rather than at the feet of capricious gods.

The nature of sin is passed on through the generations, but the spark and image of God remains. That which Buddha called Dukkha the Bible explains as humanity experiencing the consequences of separation from the source of our existence because of sin. Buddha called it a craving; theologians describe it as a god-shaped vacuum that can only be filled when the image and likeness are perfected again.

It is at this time in Genesis that we are introduced to other creatures which had previously made the choice to rebel. The origin of evil is attributed to the person of Lucifer, an Arch-angel created before the beginning of the cosmos and therefore, not a natural part of our three-dimensional world. Lucifer rebelled and, along with millions of followers, was cast out of the presence of God. Lucifer's name is changed to Satan, the 'Deceiver', and he leads the rebellion against the Creator through tempting humanity to follow his example. These creatures are called demons, *devas* in the Vedas and *deivas* in the Avestas. Demons are recognized in all ancient religious writings, but in the Bible they are never attributed as having equal power to the Creator as in Zoroastrian dualism.

Human History

Genesis records the Hebrew understanding of human history in a linear progression. After the fall of humanity the world comes under the influence of hybrid creatures who are called the Nephilim, the offspring of fallen angels and human women. As we have seen, these creatures are claimed to exist in all ancient religious writings, folklore, myths and legends.

The Bible records the event of the Great Flood and claims that God called Noah to build the Ark, a large boat which would save the animals, birds and other air-breathing creatures, and Noah's family. This event is told or recorded in over 250 different cultures worldwide, and archeological evidence, including the separation of continents, discovery of fossils and general science of 'catastrophism', offers vast amounts of evidence that The Flood occurred. Genesis covers all of the pre-flood history in just six chapters, and then moves on to give a list of the nations of the world who descended from Noah's sons, including the areas they inhabited, the cities they built, and the civilizations which came from them.

The Bible then focuses on God's solution and plan to save humanity. Abraham, a historical figure, is called to become the father of the nation through whom the entire world will be blessed and have the opportunity to be restored into a right relationship with God. Other nations such as the Babylonians, Assyrians, Persians and Egyptians, are mentioned only as they interconnect with the Nation of Hebrews (Israel) which is the central focus of God's plan of salvation. The Bible never gives us an elevated view of this nation or of its main historical characters, such as Abraham and Moses, but rather shows them 'warts and all' - their strengths and weaknesses, successes and failures.

But the Bible is not simply interested in giving us a reliable source of the human history of the Middle East. Its purpose, although not always obvious to casual readers, is to show God's preparation for His own entrance into the world of men. The Incarnation of Christ, God the Creator becoming a human being, is the underlying message of the entire Hebrew Bible, a plan which will take around 5000 years to implement.

Abraham's life is both historical and analogical. The Bible records that his wife Sarah was barren and past child-bearing age. God promised the couple a child, Abraham believed, but his wife laughed. Sarah gave Abraham her hand-maiden in an attempt to produce a child by proxy. Abraham agreed and Ishmael was born, the man who was to become the father of the Arab nations. About twelve years later Abraham was visited by three 'men'.

This meeting is considered to be a 'Christophany'; an appearance of God in physical form. In Genesis we read of the Lord walking in the Garden. Scripture, from the very beginning, speaks of God in plural terms. Elohim, one of God's names, is plural, and when God decided to create humanity He says 'let *us* make man in *our* own image'. The Bible is unique in presenting God as a Triune being - one God in three indivisible persons. Other religions have multiple gods, or gods which bear children, split apart, etc., but the Bible states that these 'gods' are merely fallen angels posing as gods in order to gain the adoration and obedience of humanity.

The very idea of a Triune God is impossible to understand in human terms. How can we conceive a being which is three in One, or One in three? Religious history gives us a multitude of gods which we can understand - gods of wind, fire, storm, and sun, emotions and actions - but nowhere except the Bible is God revealed as Triune. In the later writings of the prophets, such as Isaiah 9:6, we read of the Son of God who is also called Eternal Father, Almighty God and Wonderful Counselor, the names of God as Father and Holy Spirit. It is God the Son in His pre-incarnate form who walks in the Garden of Eden and speaks to Abraham face-to-face. It is this God the Son who becomes the Son of God, the child prophesied to be born in Bethlehem, born of a virgin, the Messiah Jesus.

Abraham lived in the city of Ur, a city excavated in the 1920s. In the center of the city was a huge Ziggurat, the remains of which still stand today, even though it is believed that it was built prior to the Great Flood.

Ziggurats were built for the worship of the gods, and child sacrifice was common in Abraham's time. God called Abraham to leave this place and gave him the land that was then called Canaan, after one of Noah's grandsons. After the birth of the promised child, Isaac, and when the boy was perhaps ten years old, God ordered Abraham to take Isaac to a mountain in the South of Canaan and offer him as a sacrifice. During the narrative Isaac is referred to as Abraham's 'only son', a reference to him as the child of the promise.

Within this story are many references to the future sacrifice of the Messiah, including the fact that the very spot on which Abraham prepared the sacrifice is the place where Jesus Christ was crucified. God did not allow Abraham to go through with the act; it was a test. But to Biblical scholars the story is one of many typologies, stories of actual events in Abraham's life which point to the future.

The rest of Genesis is history, a record of the development of a nation from the man Abraham. During this history we read of the destruction of Sodom and Gomorrah, two infamous cities where homosexuality was the norm, various battles with kings who are mentioned in other ancient texts, and finally, the story of Joseph who is sold into slavery by his jealous brothers. Joseph ends up in Egypt and, through a series of events which demonstrate his faith in God, becomes the Prime Minister of that country. During a time of extreme famine, the Hebrew people, led by Joseph's father, Israel, go to Egypt and settle there. God had warned Abraham that his descendents would live in a foreign land in slavery for 400 years. After the death of Joseph, a Pharaoh took the throne who enslaved the Hebrew people and the prophecy was lived out.

Exodus

The second book of the Bible, known as Exodus, begins with a list of the men who entered Egypt 400 years earlier. It then moves forward 400 years to the birth of the man God had chosen for the next part of His plan of salvation, the man Moses. Born a Hebrew, his mother hid him in the reeds along the shore of the Nile, as the Pharaoh had ordered the murder of Jewish boys in order to control the growth of his Hebrew slave population. Moses was found by Pharaoh's daughter and raised in the palace. At age 40 he killed a man and fled Egypt, going into the Sinai Desert where he married and became a shepherd.

Over the next 40 years he tended sheep and became very familiar with the region. One day he had an encounter with God, another Christophany. During this encounter God revealed His name as "I Am', a name Jesus used to describe Himself on several occasions about 1400 years later. Moses and his brother Aaron are sent to Egypt to demand the release of the Hebrew people. God works miracles through the two men, often using natural phenomena in supernatural ways. During this story the Pharaoh's magicians and shamans also perform supernatural deeds, and the spiritual battle comes to a climax with what is known as the Passover.

Passover is one of the most powerful typologies in Scripture. The Hebrew people are told that God will pass over the land of Egypt, and all who have not obeyed God's instructions will suffer the loss of their firstborn sons. Moses gives the people specific instructions on how to prepare for this event. The people are to select a perfect lamb, four days before the Passover, kill it in the middle of the day and break none of its bones, attach it to a forked branch with iron, and place its blood on the top and sides of their doors. To Christians, all of these signs point to the coming of Jesus Christ who was the perfect Lamb of God, who entered Jerusalem four days before Passover, who was crucified in the afternoon, was attached to a wooden cross with iron and pierced with a spear rather than His legs broken, as He was already dead.

That night, 1400 years before Christ was born, the firstborn of the Egyptians died and Pharaoh finally ordered the Jews to leave. They headed towards Sham El Sheik, and it was here that Pharaoh's elite army caught up with them when the king changed his mind about allowing them to leave. According to the story, about 2 million people followed a physical sign of God's presence, a pillar of cloud during the day and fire at night. When they arrived at the Red Sea this cloud moved behind the Hebrews and stood between them and the Egyptian army.

Moses was ordered to touch the sea with his staff; a great wind came up and parted the waves across the reef which extends across to Saudi Arabia. The Hebrew people walked across and the Pillar of Cloud followed them. Pharaoh's army charged after them as the waves returned, destroying chariots, horses and men. Since the creation of Sham El Sheik as a tourist resort, and its reef for observing tropical fish, several claims of finding ancient chariot wheels have surfaced.

This story, as mentioned earlier, is recorded in Egypt's own history. Until this time the Egyptians had been easily able to repel the Sea People who came up the Nile to attack, but without Egypt's mighty army, Egypt was vulnerable and lost much of its territory.

Law and Covenant

The Hebrew people followed God to the Mountain of Fire known today as 'Jabal Al Lawz'. It was here that God made a covenant with the people. Moses lay boundary stones around the base and warned the people that any who trespassed over the line would die. Only Moses was allowed to go up onto the mountain, the place where the presence of God met with him. The rocks around the top of Jabal Al Lawz have been darkened as if cooked in incredible heat, and yet this is not an active volcano or any such thing.

Other details mentioned in Exodus, such as the boundary stones, altar and animal pens, have also been found at this site.

Moses is given the Ten Commandments. These became the basis of the covenant law between Jehovah God and the Jewish people. Other nations had codes and laws, but the commandments and extensive laws recorded in Leviticus are the most systematic laws ever written in ancient times, covering everything from instructions for worship, sacrifices, laws on human behavior, punishments for crimes, sexual morality, farming, leasing and money lending, to the treatment of slaves and alien peoples, etc.

Much of Hebrew Law has become the basis for Western Legal practice. Hebrew Law differs from other codes as it places God as the standard for morality and practice, rather than human standards. God's covenant with Israel is conditional upon their obedience to the law. They are the only nation on the planet which is forbidden to worship or follow any other god, to make images and idols or engage in sorcery, magic and shamanism. To the God of the Hebrews, all other deities are not gods at all, but rather fallen angels posing as such - demons who will lead the people into all manner of sin.

Prophets

Other than their Law, which in itself is unique, the Hebrew people had prophets throughout their history leading up to the coming of the

Messiah. Prophets were chosen by God himself and these people were always tested. Prophets gave specific warnings of events which concluded within their own lifetimes, and if they were not 100% accurate they and their families were killed. This was to safeguard against false seers, shamans and magicians who could claim to have a message from God but lead the people into immorality and idol worship. Those prophets including Ezekiel, Isaiah, Daniel, Micah and Jeremiah, were given hundreds of specific prophecies about a Messiah King who would liberate the people from sin.

Israel had some mighty kings such as David who made Jerusalem his capital in 1000BC and Solomon, David's son, who undertook the building of the great temple. God promised another king like David. The Jews had walked away from God on many occasions, and He had allowed them to be conquered by the nations around them because of their disobedience. They waited expectantly for a king who would free them from captivity, but their leaders failed to understand the deeper meaning of the prophecies.

Isaiah foretold the peculiar means of His virgin birth and Micah the place of His birth. Isaiah foretold the purpose of His life and called Him the 'Suffering Servant', the one who would die for the sins of the people to bring liberation, not from human oppressors, but from captivity to sin. David foretold the way He would die, describing a crucifixion scene 600 years before this form of death had been invented or used.

Isaiah told of His resurrection and Joel of the new covenant God would make with both Jew and non-Jew (Gentile) alike. And then, for 400 years before His birth the prophets were silent, just as they were during the Jewish slavery in Egypt for the same length of time. The Greeks had come and gone, the Romans now ruled a great Empire, and the Jewish people waited on God to fulfill the prophecies He had given.

Points to Ponder

The Hebrew Bible, which is referred to as The Old Testament by Christians, has been the subject of intense scholarly research for centuries. It contains history, legal instructions, Psalms and adoration poems directed to God, prophecies and stories. The word 'Bible' simply means library or collection, and we recognize that the Hebrew

Bible had many authors, most of whom never met one another. As a historical text no other book has been found to have the archaeological accuracy of the Bible. The Jewish people were surrounded by other nations, interacting and even going to war with them. The writings of those nations help to authenticate many of the Bible's claims.

But perhaps the reason the Bible has been so scrutinized by scholars is the mysterious element it contains. It is all too easy to suggest that prophet authors wrote down their prophecies after events had taken place, and we do know that many events happened within these prophets' own lifetimes, but the prophecies about Jesus Christ are extremely specific, although traditional Jewish scholars have often ignored them. Prophecies, typologies and Christophanies have no scientific explanation, at least not in the way that science evaluates in a general sense.

The miracle stories told in the Exodus could be easily dismissed by skeptics if this was the only record of the event, but why would the Egyptians record something which was such an embarrassing defeat? This is just one example of why the Hebrew Bible has fascinated scholars, archaeologists and others for centuries, and will continue to do so, for many of its prophecies are about the future of the world, its steady decline towards destruction, and the Second Coming of Christ.

For further study.
Reading the Old Testament, Lawrence Boadt (Paulist Press, New York, 1984)
Old Testament Theology, Paul R. House (IVP Academic, Illinois, 1998)
A Biblical Theology of The Old Testament, Roy B. Zuck (Moody Publishers, Chicago, 1991)
The Message of The Old Testament, Mark Dever (Crossway Books Illinois, 2006)
Time for Truth, Steve Copland (E-book, Smashwords, 2012)

Chapter Ten: Greeks

The religion of the Greeks is not, strictly speaking, the myths and stories of the Greeks. The Greeks loved mythology and storytelling, and although their stories often had moral and religious implications, the gods they worshipped were not usually their god-like heroes. Stories of nymphs, centaurs, flying horses, minotaurs and griffins are commonplace, but were used to teach principles rather than draw one to veneration.

Yet, some of the mythical traditions of the Greeks have strong similarities to the legends of the Aryans, pre-flood stories, and Genesis 6. The Golden Age, for example, is the time of the Titans, a time which preceded the worship of gods such as Zeus, Aphrodite, Ares and Apollo. The Titans were huge immortal beings of incredible strength centered on the fabled city of Atlantis in the time before the Flood. There were several tribes of Titans who constantly warred with each other. Some were said to be the offspring of gods and human women, such as Kastor and Polyduekes, the heavenly twins, and Hercules, all who were believed to be sons of Zeus and his human wives.

The philosopher Plato wrote about the city of Atlantis, believing it was a pre-Flood kingdom of demi-gods who ruled the world of men, and were essentially evil. Such stories are extremely similar to the Nephilim of Genesis 6 and the Book of Enoch.

Greek Religion

In order to rightly understand Greek religion we need to recognize that philosophical ideas and religious beliefs are very closely related. Take, for example, the idea of fate or destiny. Fate is a philosophical idea which presumes that our birth, life and death have been predestined, and in the case of the Greeks, by the Three Sisters of Fate. Grace or virtue is likewise a gift under the control of three goddess figures.

The Greek Pantheon also included gods who were worshipped and feared for their power over nature and human emotions. The following are the most important:

Zeus. Zeus was believed to be the king of the gods, yet he was a created being, the son of Cronus and Rhea. He was said to punish mortals with lightning and thunder.

Poseidon. Another son of Cronus and Rhea, Poseidon was in control of the seas and earthquakes. Sailors made sacrifices to this god in exchange for good weather and protection from storms.

Eros. Eros was the god of love. He was the one who made men and women fall in love with each other and controlled such emotions.

Hera. This goddess was very important to Greek people as she had control over marriage and childbirth. Without her blessing, conception was believed to be impossible. It is thought that the very first covered temples were dedicated to her around 800BC.

Apollo. Apollo was the son of Zeus and Leto. This god had a dual nature. On the one hand he gave gifts and talents to produce music and poetry, whilst on the other hand he could send plagues, offer healing, light and knowledge. He is the god of the philosophers, the one who opens men's eyes to wisdom, but also the one who destroys those who disobey him.

Athena. Athena is the patron goddess of Athens. She is the goddess of wisdom, warfare, architecture and crafts, law and justice, mathematics and strategy. As such, she was worshipped by the philosophers, politicians, teachers and magistrates, builders and craftsmen.

Artemis. The temple in Ephesus, built for the worship of Artemis, had 121 columns and was considered to be one of the Seven Wonders of the World. Although portrayed as a huntress and believed to be the goddess of wild animals and hunting, she was venerated more so for her powers over childbirth, virginity and disease among women. For the Ephesians, to allow discredit of her would bring disaster to the city, especially to its women.

Aphrodite. She is the goddess of seduction, erotic love, beauty, and conception, but not concerned with marriage and childbirth. In the temple cults, worship attributed to her was conducted by having sex with the temple prostitutes. This practice was believed to increase fertility.

Isis. Although originally an Egyptian goddess, Isis became very popular with Greeks. She was thought to be able to forgive sins and was the friend of slaves, rulers, the downtrodden, the wealthy and aristocratic. She is also the goddess of magic and the casting of spells.

Dionysus. As the god of wine and fertility, Dionysus represents both joy and chaos, two elements associated with drunkenness.

Greek Religious Philosophy

For the Greeks, especially during the latter time of the Empire, philosophy played a much larger role than mythology and influenced other religions. A good deal of Greek philosophical thought was used to explain difficult ideas within Christianity, and even the New Testament writers themselves borrowed from the Greeks to explain aspects of the gospels. In this section we will examine some of the most influential of the philosophers and their contributions.

Socrates (469-399 BC)
Almost everything we know of Socrates comes from those who wrote about him, especially Plato and Aristotle. His influence on Western thinking comes from his dialectic method of inquiry. Problems are broken down and examined through a series of questions. Those answers which reveal contradictions are discarded.

This formula was used to examine ethical and mathematical issues, and is the basis of scientific method. One begins with a hypothesis and rejects or builds on it as it is proven or disproved. The dialectical method was used to test one's beliefs and the validity of beliefs. Socrates believed that the pursuit of individual virtue was the highest ideal, both for the individual and society.

Plato (428-348 BC)
Plato was a student of Socrates who presented his philosophical ideas in a series of *dialogues*. Two of his major contributions to Christian thinking concern his idea of Logos, and immortality.

Logos (The Word)

Plato taught that the gods, their power and influence, could be portrayed in a hierarchal structure in the shape of a pyramid. On the very tip was the Logos, and beneath, various other gods and daemons. The Logos is the essence of the Divine and also the physical manifestation of the Divine through which the Divine acts in creation, time and space. The Apostle John borrowed this idea to speak about the incarnation of Jesus Christ. Logos is translated as 'The Word' and the first verses of John's gospel read this way.

> "In the beginning was the Word (Logos) and the Word was with God, and the Word was God. He was with God in the beginning. Through Him all things were made; without Him nothing was made that has been made...(v14) The Word became flesh and dwelt among us. We have seen His glory, the glory of the one and only Son, who came from the Father, full of grace and truth."

God, the uncreated One, is the Logos, immortal, unseen and dwelling beyond time and space, the one referred to as "The Ancient of Days". Plato believed that the Logos could manifest Himself in physical form. For John, this form was Jesus Christ.

Immortality

Plato also taught that the human soul is immortal. Immortality means 'that which cannot be destroyed', that which is beyond the material world and therefore unaffected by it in terms of death or destruction. For Plato, the human soul was a part of the essence of the Logos, not simply an image or likeness, but of the same essence and therefore immortal, indestructible. In the gospels, Jesus rejects this idea (Matthew 10:28), as did the Apostle Paul (1st Timothy 6:16).

Strictly speaking, the Bible states that immortality is a gift from God, given to those who seek it (Romans 2:7) and only through faith in the saving power of Jesus Christ. Those who reject this salvation are brought out of Hades (a temporary place of torment and suffering), united with their bodies, and judged. They are then cast into the 'Lake of Fire' where they experience the 'second death' (Revelation 20: 11-15).

Plato's ideas were adopted by the influential writer, Origen of Alexandria (185-254AD), whose theology was quoted extensively by the heretic Arius, a Roman Catholic priest who claimed Jesus was not equal to God the Father. This view ignited the Arian Controversy and led to the development of the Christian Creeds. Modern day Jehovah's Witnesses still teach the views of Arius.

Aristotle (384-322BC)

Aristotle's influence cannot be overstated, covering many topics such as logic, physics, poetry, ethics, art, biology, government, politics and zoology. He is considered the first philosopher to formulate a systematic method of formal logic. Many consider him to be the world's first real scientist. It was Aristotle that first documented a thesis on 'causality', naming four main causes for everything. This work became the basis of the late Medieval Scholastic movement premise of God as the 'First Cause', put forward by Thomas Aquinas.

Aristotle was also the first to document natural history. He observed, experimented and wrote about animals, fish and birds, and wrote several books which still survive.

Aristotle differed from his teacher Plato in his understanding of the human soul. For Aristotle, the soul, which he described in three ways, was the whole person. In this sense, the body is a physical reflection of the soul. His works were largely unknown during the Medieval Period (Dark Ages) within Roman Catholic Christianity until discovered again after the Renaissance. However, during the Medieval Period he was studied by Islamic scholars.

Epicurus (341-270BC)

Epicurus equated good and evil with pleasure and pain. The goal of life is simply to avoid pain and enjoy. He did believe in the gods of the Greeks, but that they had no interest in humanity, and therefore, that people brought unnecessary pain upon themselves by trying to appease them. He also denied any idea of an afterlife. Once we are dead we feel nothing and cease to exist; therefore, it is foolish to fear death.

Epicurus is also attributed with the 'Epicurean paradox', a trilemna argument. It proposes the following:

Is God willing to prevent evil, but not able? Then He is not omnipotent (all powerful).
Is He able to prevent evil, but not willing? Then He is malevolent (evil).

If He is both willing and able, then how can evil exist?
If He is neither willing nor able, then why call Him God?

The Epicurean argument is still popular, especially with atheists, today. On the surface it may seem to be a logical paradox which is self-explanatory; however, it fails to recognize other possibilities. God may be all powerful and all loving but allow evil to exist for a time in order to achieve a greater purpose than what can be known in the immediate present. If, like Epicurus, we believe that there is no life after death, then his paradox is valid.

However if God has allowed evil to exist in order to test the hearts of humanity through freedom to choose, with the view that their actions will determine their eternal existence, then his argument is false. A loving, all powerful God, who hates evil could allow it because in doing so it determines those people who long to have immortality free from evil.

Points to Ponder

Greek philosophical thought has provided much of the foundations of modern science, analysis, biology, physics and mathematics. Its contributions to religion are also predominant, especially through the writings of Plato, Aristotle and Epicurus. Plato's claim of the soul's immortality became accepted by the Roman Catholic Church and influenced the way that Scripture has been interpreted ever since.

If the soul cannot be destroyed, then eternal torment and suffering in hell must be without end. This idea coined a new phrase, 'eternal death', a term not in the Bible. There are as many verses in the Bible which speak of eternal destruction as there are of eternal torment. Biblical scholars cannot make these seeming contradictions unite unless they jettison their Platonic philosophy about the immortality of the soul.

The Bible uses words which are translated as eternal and forever to simply mean 'outside of time'. Our material universe is governed by time and space; even our hearts beat to its rhythm. Yet the Bible can state that a person can be in Hades (one word for hell where there is suffering) forever, and yet that existence ends.

In other words, a soul which enters Hades has no concept of time, they are outside of it, But God can bring them out of Hades and end their existence 'forever' in Gehenna, a word which means a place of absolute destruction. Jesus never confused the two terms. When he spoke of suffering He always used Hades, and when He warned of destruction, He used Gehenna.

These ideas are difficult for us to grasp because it is almost impossible for us to entertain infinity, and because the Bible always uses analogies to describe places such as hell. Is hell a place or a mode of being? Is it possible for human beings to imagine a 'place' which is beyond our three-dimensional understanding?

The Book of Revelation, with its colorful imagery, is a classic example of using such imagery to explain concepts beyond our human experience.

Chapter Eleven: Romans

The Great orator Cicero once said of the Roman Empire that; 'if we compared our national characteristics with those of other nations, we are their equals and in some respects inferior, yet in the sense of religion, that is, reverence of the gods, we are greatly superior'. Cicero's statement sums up the importance of the gods to the Roman mind. The Romans conquered Greece around 146 BC and adopted many aspects of Greek culture into its own. Rome was a military empire, especially in its beginnings, but its policy of integrating other cultures' philosophies and cultural superiority meant that Rome, as an empire, became very diverse.

Greek religion had a great influence. Romans incorporated the gods of the Greeks; indeed they considered that the Greeks' gods and their own were much the same but with different names. Zeus was associated with Jupiter, Hera with Juno, Poseidon with Neptune, Aphrodite with Venus, etc. The Romans accepted new gods into their Pantheon whenever they conquered another nation. The conquered peoples were allowed to continue worshipping their traditional gods, but the Empire insisted that all Romans give veneration to Rome's traditional deities. The reason for this lies in the fact that Romans believed their military success was a direct consequence or reward for their faithfulness in worship and veneration. If they allowed people to ignore their gods, they would risk the wrath of those gods bringing disaster to the Empire.

Romans had a strong belief in an afterlife, a concept which was very similar to life here on earth, but where perfect justice was available to those who had been wronged. Whether or not they believed in the immortality of the soul before the influence of Plato is unclear, but it became a foundational belief after conquering the Greeks. In simple terms, the Roman afterlife is about merit. Warriors who honored Rome and their gods in battle received a place in Paradise after drinking an elixir which took away memories of their earthly life. Ordinary citizens who did not distinguish themselves continued a similar existence to that on earth, but those who had really offended the gods were sent to Tatarus (hell) where they were punished for a time deemed appropriate.

Roman Temple Worship

The temples of ancient Rome were busy places. Almost every type of food imaginable was taken to be blessed by various gods. Many sacrifices occurred in an area outside of the temple, especially those which were used to deify meat. Animals were killed near the temple and the meat blessed before being taken for sale in the marketplace; therefore, some temples acted as a modern day abattoir. This particular practice became a problem for the early Christian believers as all meat had been sacrificed to what Christians considered demons or idols. The Christians' refusal to worship Rome's gods was one of the contributing factors in the persecutions against believers. They were labeled as atheists and believed to be offending the gods.

To the Roman mind no important decision or part of life could be embarked upon without a sacrifice to the god associated with that particular undertaking. Weddings must be approved by the gods and children could not be expected without the proper sacrifice to a goddess. Wealth and prosperity came only to those blessed by the gods; good health or diseases were handed out in relation to faithfulness.

Fertility goddesses were prevalent in Roman cities as children were seen as vitally important. The emphasis on sexual rites led to the establishment of hundreds of temples dedicated exclusively to pagan sexual practices without moral restraint. In this, Roman culture was a contradiction in terms. Romans had strict rules about adultery, whilst at the same time both husbands and wives would frequent the temples of Diana, Aphrodite, Venus and Isis to perform sexual acts with male and female prostitutes. Women were less inclined to visit such temples, but it was considered an obligation for men from the time of puberty.

Temple prostitutes were considered to be sacred vessels of the goddess herself, and the more debauched the sexual activities were, the more the couple would be blessed. Roman men wanted sons, for daughters were often seen as a burden rather than blessing. It was the Romans who invented abortion, firstly in the temples. A witch or seer would dangle a sacred amulet above the expectant mother's abdomen. If the amulet swung in a clockwise direction the woman was having a male child, and if anticlockwise, the pregnancy was terminated, often resulting in the death of both mother and child.

Girls who were born in temples were raised as prostitutes, trained in massage and erotic forms of sexual pleasure. Boys were sold as slaves, often to wealthy landowners who had them trained as gladiators in schools especially for preparing warriors for the games which had become so popular in the Empire. The owner of the gladiator received a percentage of the winnings if his gladiator was victorious, in a similar way that people invest in racehorses today.

The Imperial Cult

As Rome increased its territories and the number of its gods, it moved from being a Republic towards a republican dictatorship.

Rome initially had senators and *princeps*. A princep was initially like a principle senator, a wealthy and very influential man whose vote in the senate held more weight than others. However, as military conquests expanded, imperators with senatorial connections came to be seen as heroes and leaders chosen by the gods. Victorious imperators had always received great honor, but this increased to something more.

The Julian dynasty is a case in point. The Julio/Claudian Princeps, who were initially seen as simply blessed vessels of the gods, came to be viewed as divine emperors in themselves and so the imperial cult was born. Whereas before an Emperor was subject to the Senate to a certain degree, now he was seen as a god in living form and, therefore, worthy of worship. Previous princeps had only been rewarded with divine status after their deaths, but the idea of a living god became the norm from the 1st century onwards.

It is thought by some scholars that the introduction of the imperial cult was influenced by civilizations such as the Egyptian. Cleopatra, who was involved in taking the side of Mark Antony against Augustus, considered herself a living reflection of Isis and was worshipped as such. When Mark Antony met with her in Tarsus, a meeting which began both their romance and downfall, he represented himself as a god.

His defeat thrust the victor into divine status and the idea became an established part of Roman belief. If a person refused to worship the Emperor, swear to his divinity and fail to make appropriate sacrifices, such a one was considered a traitor of the Empire and subject to the death penalty. It isn't difficult to imagine how this policy became a major concern for Christianity.

The Emperor Nero, knowing that Christians refused to worship him, used them as scapegoats when he secretly ordered the burning of a section of Rome. Nero wanted space to erect a new palace for himself and a temple with a statue some thirty meters in height. The fire spread throughout Rome, destroying a large percentage of the city, so the Emperor turned suspicion away from himself by blaming a people considered to be atheists and traitors. This was the beginning of formal and universal persecution against the Christian church which lasted over 300 years.

Mystery Cults

Throughout the Roman Empire the mystery religions of conquered nations were often adapted and practiced by Roman citizens. The god Mithras, which we have encountered in previous religions, became a popular god, especially amongst Roman soldiers. Mithras was not considered the god of war - that honor went to Mars; however, Mithras was able to give his worshippers supernatural powers. The rites of Mithraism are difficult to discover as this cult was extremely secretive; however, some of its practices have been recorded, especially by Roman soldiers who left the cult on being converted to Christianity.

An initiate was tested with extreme torture, usually three times. This was to ensure that he was capable of keeping the secrets of the cult under duress. If he passed the tests, then a ceremony was performed in a Mithraeum, a place of worship usually in a large cave underground. Initiates had to lie in shallow graves in front of a live bull that was shackled.

The Pater, the highest ranked member of the cult, held a sacred knife above the initiate's heart as the new worshipper bound his life to Mithras. As he spoke the words, his body lifted from the ground and into the knife involuntarily. This act, which usually would have brought death, imparted the spirit of Mithras into the new recruit. The bull was then slain and its blood sprayed out and over the initiates, 'baptizing' them in its blood. This act symbolized that they had died to their old lives and been born into a new life dedicated to their god.

There were seven ranks within Mithraism. Practice included meditation, animal and human sacrifices, the drinking of soma and levitation, all similar to the ancient practices of the Aryans. High ranking members were said to have superhuman strength and be almost invincible on the field of battle. Each enemy warrior slain was a sacrifice to Mithras.

Family Gods

Romans, like the Greeks, believed in a hierarchy of gods. Near the bottom of this pyramid were the *lares* and *penates* which are sometimes referred to as household gods. Lares were always associated with a particular location which they watched over, such as roads, towns, livestock, forests, etc. It was also thought that ancestors had become Lares who watched over the family. Almost all Roman homes had a niche in the wall where small statues of their household gods were kept, prayed to, and offered sacrifices and gifts.

Lares and penates were sometimes referred to as 'familiar spirits', that is, spirits which were familiar with the family in which they were worshipped. Tiny figurines, representing members of the family who had died, were kept in the niche. Presumably, these were also able to influence the greater gods because they were in the spirit realm.

The Roman Conversion to Christianity

For almost three centuries the early Christian Church was persecuted by the Roman Empire. Sometimes persecution was localized and at others, universal. Nero started the process, but later Emperors waged war on Christians. The Empire was suffering various defeats, especially on its Northern Frontier, and for Roman minds this meant that the gods were angry. Christians refused to pay homage to idols or the Emperor; therefore, they were labeled as atheists, and dangerous for the health of Rome. Martyrdom was common, for thousands refused to reject Christ even to horrifying deaths in the arenas, dungeons and crucifixion.

The more the Romans murdered them, the more the Church grew, for the testimony of the dying had a profound effect on those who watched. One story is told of a young Roman soldier who had given his life to Christ and was serving on the Northern Front near the Rhine. After a long march they arrived back at their garrison beside a frozen lake. Before entering the warmth, every soldier had to give obeisance to Mars, the god of war, for their success that day. The young Christian refused.

His centurion, livid, had him stripped naked and sent to stand on the ice until he changed his mind. Mars could not be offended or the battle would not go so well the next day. The centurion left men guarding the shivering figure and went to bed. In the morning he discovered seventeen Roman soldiers frozen to death on that lake. According to the legend, the young man sang songs to Jesus as he was dying. His fearless testimony was so powerful that sixteen others converted to Christianity before the night was done.

Early in the 4th century the Emperor Constantine decided to declare the Roman Empire Christian, indeed, the state religion. Legend has it that he saw the sign of a cross while in a battle and heard the words 'in this sign conquer', or some such thing. Constantine never converted to Christianity; indeed he remained the head priest of the pagan temples and was reluctantly baptized on his death bed. Constantine wanted a united Empire, and Christianity was impossible to stamp out. In Christian terms, his 'conversion' marks the beginning of the Dark Ages.

Chapter Twelve: Christianity

The beginnings of Christianity are, for Christians at least, rooted in the Scriptures of the Hebrew people, the Old Testament. As we discovered in the Hebrew Bible, the Jewish people were expecting a Messiah, one they perceived as a liberator from their centuries of subjugation to the more powerful nations around them. Although many of the prophecies spoke of the Messiah as a spiritual savior, these were often overlooked in their Rabbis' hope for freedom.

The last true prophet who spoke to Israel was Malachi. His voice was the last time Jehovah would speak to them through prophets for 430 years, the exact time they were enslaved in the land of Egypt. During these silent years many would-be messiahs rose up in the name of Jehovah with the intentions of raising an army. These men interpreted the Scriptures from a selective perspective, taking only those prophecies which spoke of a new king who would be a descendent of David, the man God used to make Israel an independent nation.

David's son Solomon was the most powerful king in the Middle East during his reign, and certainly the wealthiest. Those were the glory days of Israel as a nation. But Solomon was led astray by his heathen wives; he turned away from the Law of Moses and worshipped the Baal's and Ashtorah, the goddess of fertility. Solomon's sin had terrible consequences. The Jews were led astray by various kings and God sent other nations against them to call them to repentance, fulfilling the curses of the covenant they made with Him.

By the time Jesus Christ was born many messiahs had come and gone. Judas Galilaeus, a charismatic leader, was one such man. He drew an army to himself, preaching against paying the Roman taxes, a thing he saw as blasphemy towards God. He had many followers, but Rome sent its own army, and with the help of their puppet Jewish ruler Herod, slaughtered Galilaeus and his followers without mercy. The Jewish leaders, men who saw themselves as responsible for the spiritual welfare of the nation, were rightly suspicious of new messiah figures, so when Jesus Christ made Himself known, and His fame spread through the miraculous healings he performed, they watched Him closely.

Micah 5:2 prophesied that the coming ruler of Israel, whose 'origins are eternal', would be born in the small town of Bethlehem Ephrathah. Jesus was known as Jesus of Nazareth, for this was where He was raised. Nazareth had a poor reputation, so when the rulers learned of His being raised there, they were inclined to immediately dismiss Him, for there were no Scriptures which supported the idea of the Messiah coming from such a town.

Jesus was something of an enigma, a living mystery for the Pharisees and Sanhedrin, the ruling men of Israel. On the one hand He did miracles which were impossible for them to deny, miracles such as healing leprosy, a disease which, it was believed, only God Himself could heal. On the other hand, He didn't bow and scrape to them as other people did. The Pharisees commanded respect and fear. They had the power to have a person excommunicated - thrown out of the temple, and basically out of the community of God's people. Jesus challenged them openly, and in doing so, turned many of them into enemies.

The Laws of Moses were not difficult to understand, but over the centuries Rabbis had added their own interpretations to them. Moses wrote 'keep the Sabbath Day holy', basically a commandment meaning to stop working and honor God on this day. But the Pharisees had written screeds on what 'work' meant, and it was *their* interpretation which was forced upon the common man. Jesus contradicted their interpretation, taking the Law back to its heart, its soul. His teachings uplifted the people but infuriated the Jewish rulers, for their authority was undermined. Therefore, they accused Him of not keeping the Law of Moses, a claim He denied. Even before His first year of ministry had ended there were Pharisees who wanted Him dead, and any thought of these men searching the Scriptures or seeking answers about where He was born was long past.

Jesus' Ministry

John the Baptist, the hermit prophet/preacher who called the people to repentance, was himself prophesied to come and 'prepare the way of the Lord'. He recognized Jesus as the 'Lamb of God who takes away the sins of the world', and this was on the day that Jesus began His ministry. Jesus called twelve men to be His closest disciples and for three years they walked with Him, watching, learning and speculating. The disciples admit that they didn't understand His message or purpose until after He was crucified. Like their spiritual leaders, they expected Him to go up to Jerusalem and claim the Jewish throne, declare Himself king, and send the Romans packing. They knew the stories of previous messiah figures who'd died before their time, so when Jesus was crucified they were thrown into confusion and doubt.

Jesus preached a message of the Kingdom of God. He spoke about this Kingdom as being present and future. It was present because He was present, and future because He would return to His Father and send the Holy Spirit to establish this Kingdom within the souls of believers. The four gospels record His ministry in detail but were written several decades after His resurrection. It is within the pages of the gospels that we learn that He was born in Bethlehem and fulfilled the many prophesies about Him, including those which foretold His death and resurrection.

For Christian scholars, the message of Jesus is consistent with the many typologies and prophesies within the Hebrew Bible. The Laws of Moses had extremely strict requirements for sacrifices to God. The concepts of redemption, atonement, forgiveness, etc., were taught by the priests. These sacrifices were part of the covenant with Israel, but they pointed forwards to a new covenant, one which would give participants the power and motivation to keep the Law and have a different type of relationship with God.

In general terms, Jewish people had a reverent fear of God. God was holy and unapproachable. Jesus spoke of His Father in a new way. He portrayed God in a way that Jewish ears had never heard before, emphasizing that God wanted people to draw close to Him. The people didn't understand how that could be possible, and it was only after His death and resurrection that His disciples understood that the barriers which stood between sinners and a holy God had been destroyed by Christ offering Himself as a sacrifice for sin.

Sometimes Jesus' words are difficult to understand, for He always taught using parables - stories with a meaning which pointed to a certain area of His message. Scholars recognize that Jesus was preparing the world for the new covenant, and in this sense, He was always pointing forwards. The disciples were not 'Christians' before the death and resurrection of Jesus; technically, they were still under the old covenant, but about 50 days after this event the new covenant was ushered in when the Holy Spirit came to dwell within believers for the first time.

Christianity: The First Years

The Book of Acts records the 'Day of Pentecost', the day when the first Christians were 'reborn'. For them, it was as if their eyes had been opened for the first time. This is the supernatural element of Christianity, a mysterious experience which millions have testified to. Acts records the apostles preaching the gospel, as they understood it, but it is pretty clear that they were learning as they went along in some respects.

What was extremely disconcerting for the Jewish rulers was the fact that Jesus followers seemed to be taking up where He had left off. Peter, John, Philip and others were performing amazing miracles just as Jesus had done. According to the gospels, the Pharisees had bribed the Roman soldiers to say that Jesus' disciples stole His body. They were well aware of His claim that He would rise again from death, so when His body disappeared, they spread these rumors.

On top of this were the testimonies of people who had seen hundreds of previously dead people walking the streets of Jerusalem when Christ was crucified, and over 500 people claiming they had seen the risen Lord Himself. This was a totally unexpected situation for the religious rulers, for they had managed to get the crowd to yell for Jesus' death when the Roman Procurator Pontius Pilate had offered them the choice of having one prisoner released, Barabbas or Jesus. Not only did they have the apostles themselves to contend with, but many who had previously decided that Jesus must be a false messiah on the grounds that He had been killed by the Romans before a huge crowd.

They took action immediately and tried everything they could to stop the preaching of the gospel. The apostles were ordered to be silent, were arrested, and before Christianity was a year old, the first person had been murdered for proclaiming Jesus Christ as the Lord and Messiah. They engaged the help of a zealous young Pharisee by the name of Saul of Tarsus. Saul, by all accounts, was well on his way to becoming one of the Seventy Rulers of Israel and perhaps even had the High Priest's position in his aspirations. He was given authority to go house to house and city to city arresting Christians, torturing them, and on occasions, putting them to death.

On his way to Damascus Saul had an encounter with Christ which changed his life from persecutor to apostle. Skeptics have a difficult time trying to understand what could make a man like Saul give up his ambitions as a Pharisee and join a Jewish sect that was hated throughout Judea. No one had tried to convert him, and it is certain he wasn't seeking to join the ranks of Christianity. His name was changed to Paul, and it is through the incredible passion, education, and remarkable intellect of this man that Christian theology was explained and documented for the first time.

Christian Theology

For Paul, to become a Christian is a life-changing experience which produces a changed life; anything less than this is a false faith or different gospel. Paul was an incredibly well-educated man, a polyglot who spoke several languages, had been trained in the Torah, Greek philosophy and the best school of the Pharisees. He was also a very independent man. Rather than going back to Jerusalem, where his life would have been in danger, and learning from the disciples who had walked with Jesus, he isolated himself and studied the Hebrew Scriptures. According to his own accounts, he received the insights he called 'his gospel' directly from Jesus Himself via Divine Revelation.

For Paul, Jesus Christ fulfilled the Law of Moses, in the sense that the entire debt of sin had been paid through the sacrifice of Jesus on the cross. Through His resurrection, Jesus had destroyed Satan's power over death and opened the door for ordinary people to have an intimate relationship with God. Paul referred to Jesus as Lord, a term which means God. In order to experience the new birth that God promised, a person must believe on Christ as Lord and Savior absolutely and exclusively. For Paul, this meant trusting in Christ alone to have the power to save. For Jewish minds this was difficult, and even absurd.

What about the Law of Moses? What about human contribution? For Paul, Christ had rendered the old covenant under the law obsolete. He believed that the Law was given as a tutor, to teach the problem of sin, and also to show us how hopelessly impossible it was to be perfected by human effort. Paul called for Jews to rely totally on

Christ for salvation apart from the Law. For Gentiles, such as the Greeks he preached to in Roman cities, Paul preached the same message, only it was a message calling them to completely cast away their old gods, superstitions and beliefs and believe on Christ for salvation. Throughout his letters Paul uses the Hebrew Scriptures, Greek philosophy and even poetry to explain the gospel he preached.

Of course there were many who dabbled in Christianity, both Jew and Gentile. Many saw the miracles that Paul and the apostles performed, heard the message and felt a call to respond, but leaving their old ways behind was too much to let go. Some Jews, which Paul called Judaisers, taught that Christians must also keep the Mosaic Law. Paul adamantly opposed them and said their gospel was utterly wrong. Some Gentile Christians tried to continue their habit of visiting the pagan temples, even participating in using the services of temple prostitutes. Paul rebuked them.

Paul believed that those who were filled with the Spirit would produce the 'fruits of the Spirit'. In a sense this was proof positive that a person was a genuine Christian. The fruits of the Spirit, listed in Galatians 5, are concerned with the ongoing transformation of a person's character and morality. He also put a great emphasis on the teaching that those who had surrendered their lives to Christ, by faith in His ability to save, were no longer citizens of this world, but rather belonged to Christ as citizens of heaven. For those who had experienced this mysterious new birth, Paul's teachings were not ideas of theology, but an everyday reality.

Early Church Practice

We know a great deal about early Church practice, not only from the Bible, but from Roman documents as well. From the beginning of universal Christian persecution under the Emperor Nero around 64AD, records were often kept of interrogations and letters sent back and forth from Emperors to subordinates. Some of these have survived through the centuries. Details about Christian worship and practice are recorded. The Church didn't use public buildings but met in homes. For those first few decades these people had scant access to the Old Testament Scriptures, and it wasn't until around thirty years after the Church's beginnings that the first letters of Paul began to be copied and circulated. So what did they do in these services?

1st Corinthians records the phenomena called gifts of the Spirit, a phenomena which still occurs today, especially in countries which have outlawed Christianity and where circumstances are similar to the early Church regarding the access of Bibles. Through the Holy Spirit, some Christians were given the ability to 'prophesy'. This form of prophesy was not the foretelling of future events, but more like a sermon or message directly from God. Often, these people spoke in human languages they had never learned, the 'gift of tongues', and others were given the gift of interpretation. Those listening were also filled with the same Spirit and had a form of spiritual discernment to know the truth or not of what was being said.

The Bible lists many different spiritual gifts including miracles, all of which were present and operating in the early Church. Those with musical gifts wrote songs which were sung as offerings of thankfulness to God, and often had lyrics which reinforced fundamental beliefs about Christ and what He had achieved on the cross. On top of this was the practice of sacraments. Those who had given their lives to Christ were baptized in water - not a sprinkling of water on the head, but a full immersion in a river or sea. This act represented going down into a grave and rising again into a new life, a death and resurrection. Baptism was also a public affair, a testimony that this person was a Christian, despite the dangers ever-present in times of persecution.

Prayer and communion were practiced by groups of Christians, often meeting several times a week. Jesus instituted the sacrament of communion (Eucharist) on the last night He was with His disciples. On that occasion He broke bread and handed around a cup of wine, symbols of His body and blood which were to be given as a sacrifice for sin. He instructed His disciples to do this in remembrance of His death.

The Institutionalized Church

Within two hundred years of Christianity the Church had a form of hierarchy. Leaders were given names such as bishop, and the individual teachings of bishops influenced their flocks. In various places the mysterious element of being born again began to be replaced by forms and traditions. Rules for Christian conduct were written and circulated and, for many, Christianity became a religion, an intellectual rather than mystical union through the Holy Spirit. The letters and gospels of the apostles were copied and circulated, and formed the New Testament, and as these became more accessible, so they began to replace the gifts of prophesy and interpretation.

Alongside this was the problem of heresy. Even within the apostle's lifetimes, some, such as Simon Magus, the father of Gnosticism, had begun to teach doctrines which contradicted and perverted the gospel. Gnosticism was one of the earliest and most prevalent - a doctrine which taught that all matter was evil and only spiritual things good. Under this Zoroastrian idea, Jesus' body was said to be only an apparition, for Jesus couldn't have a real body.

The consequences of such a teaching were far-reaching. If Jesus' body was not real, then He was not really a human being, and therefore, could not be a substitute who bore human sins on the cross. The apostles taught that Jesus was both God and man. As a human being, born of a human mother, He was subject to the same weaknesses and temptations as us, and could therefore empathize with our human nature. As God, He can lift believers to the very throne of God Himself.

Gnosticism spread through the Churches, its teachings emphasizing a form of secret knowledge given to its leaders. Angelic visions and revelations were common, and for those who had been involved with pagan mysticism and the worship of angels, it was very appealing. The Gnostics produced their own versions of the gospels, including the gospel of Thomas, which claimed Jesus murdered a boy of about eight when He was a similar age, and others which claimed Jesus was married, possibly to Mary Magdalene.

In the early 4th Century the Roman Emperor Constantine decided to make Christianity the State Religion. Constantine's decision was never based on a spiritual desire or search for truth, but rather, to unite the Empire. Rome had been trying to eliminate Christianity for almost 300 years, unsuccessfully, and it is estimated that up to 15% of the Empire was Christian by 312AD. In 313AD Constantine issued the Edict of Milan which made Christianity a legal religion and later, the only legal religion. Constantine remained the head of the pagan religion but presided over all matters concerning the Church, setting the precedent of an Emperor being the head of Christianity.

At this time in Church history the Arian Controversy was in full swing. This controversy concerned the theological issue of the

Divinity of Christ. The Arians, who held similar beliefs to the Jehovah's Witnesses today, taught that Jesus was not equal to God, but a created being. This was the second most influential heresy to spread throughout the Church since Gnosticism. If Christ was not God, how could He save, for only God can save a sinner? Constantine ordered a council and the first of the Christian creeds was drawn up in Nicaea, declaring the full Divinity of Christ.

The 'conversion' of Constantine marked the beginning of what many still refer to as 'The Dark Ages'. Pagan temples were converted into Churches and Romans were forced to reject their beloved gods and worship Jesus Christ. Most were uneducated and services were conducted by priests in Latin, a language that the majority couldn't understand. People continued to worship their Roman gods in secret, but attended Church to receive the sacrament of communion which was basically compulsory. Within a short space of time the percentage of 'born again' Christians was tiny, and Christianity became a religion of power and fear.

Two erroneous doctrines became the tools which forced people into submission to the Empire's new religion. One was the idea that humans are born sinners, that is, that from birth we are under the penalty of sin and going to hell. The Bible makes a distinction between a sinful nature, the capacity and inclination to sin, and sin itself, a conscious rebellious act. Biblically, we are born with a sin nature, and this nature leads us into sin.

Incidentally, the word translated as 'sin nature' and 'flesh' in the New Testament is the Greek word 'sarx'. The Bible states that Jesus was born with this same nature (John 1:14), yet He never surrendered to its power and sinned. Having a nature with the capacity to sin does not make one a 'born sinner'.

The doctrine of being a born sinner meant that we had inherited the *guilt* of Adam's actual sin, and were responsible for it, without the actual act of sin. Therefore, children were baptized as soon as possible after birth, for an unbaptized child who died would have no chance of being in heaven, according to this doctrine.

The other doctrine was taken from Plato's theory of the immortality of the human soul. If the soul could not be destroyed, and the person died unbaptized, then that soul would be tortured and tormented forever in a fiery hell without hope of this punishment ending. Pictures depicting sinners in hell were painted on the walls inside

Church buildings, the so-called 'doom paintings', and even for the uneducated, these were understood clearly. Jesus was portrayed watching demons ripping sinners apart, cooking them in oil, killing them and bringing them back to life, horrific scenes of excruciating torture. Most of the earliest paintings have faded or been destroyed, but the two English examples of late medieval art below are still discernable.

Christ was to be feared, for He was portrayed as God's instrument of punishment to any who disobeyed the institutionalized church's commands.

Within the schools of theology, the question was raised about Jesus' human nature. How did He escape being born as a sinner, for if He was a sinner He couldn't save anyone, but would need salvation Himself? It amazes me that these theologians seem to have completely neglected to check the Greek words within the New Testament on this issue. Perhaps the reason for this neglect lies in the fact that the Roman Catholic Church had declared the Latin language as sacred, and studying Greek was basically abandoned until the Renaissance hundreds of years later.

It was decided that Mary, His mother, was born sinless, herself being an immaculate conception as Jesus was.

The logical conclusion to all this was that Mary must be equal to Christ, and before long, pagan people who had been forced into Christianity had a new goddess in the form of Mary. Romans were used to changing their goddesses' names, and Mary became the one to pray to - the one who might speak to her judgmental, merciless Son on a sinner's behalf. The young virgin, who called God her Savior, became equal to God and crowned as the 'Queen of Heaven'. The RCC denied the many verses in the New Testament which say she went on to have at least five other children, taught that she died a virgin, and claimed she was as perfect as God, raising statues to her which are revered.

This is somewhat of an over-simplification; nevertheless, it is very accurate, although these doctrines evolved through the centuries. The Popes became the Emperors after the fall of the Empire and ruled millions. Their power was absolute and their words unquestionable, for they portrayed and taught that they, and they alone, were the living representatives of Christ on earth.

Within 500 years Christianity had changed dramatically from an individual relationship with Christ, through a mystical experience of being born again, to an institutionalized religion with a mission to rule the world. This is not to say that there were some who did experience new birth, but rather, that the majority who went by the name of Christian had been forced to adhere intellectually to a religion and God they neither knew nor loved. Roman Catholicism spread throughout the known world, into Britain and Northern Europe, led by missionaries and armies. Conquered peoples were forced to believe or die.

But Roman Catholicism was to meet a challenge to its plan of world domination. In a cave in the Middle East a young man was seeking a spiritual experience using the age-old practice of a form of soma. He was to become the leader and prophet of a new religion which would use violence as a means of conversion - the religion of Islam.

Points to Ponder

From a purely spiritual standpoint, one could argue that Satanic forces were trying to destroy Christianity from its beginnings, firstly, from within, using Gnostic beliefs. Simon Magus' father was Persian and no doubt Simon was thoroughly versed in Zoroastrianism. Gnosticism's ideas were extremely similar to this ancient religion, but also had the appeal of mystery and self-development. The great early Christian apologists such as Irenaeus wrote volumes against this early heresy and eventually seem to have overcome it.

Then came the attack from outside. The persecutions were designed to completely eradicate this young faith before it could really take root. For nearly three hundred years Christians were murdered, yet persecution had the opposite effect. During those years of persecution the theology of the Church remained, to a large degree, pure and true to the New Testament. People counted the cost of giving their lives to

Christ, for the chances were that such a conversion could mean a short life and painful death. There are few Christian hypocrites around when crazed Emperors are demanding your denial of Christ or death.

Onto the stage came Constantine. Was this man's 'conversion' a miracle of God, or a master stroke of Satan? For me, it was the latter. Through the Roman Catholic Church of the Medieval Period, the fundamental tenants of Christianity were lost and perverted. No longer were people called to be born again and filled with the Holy Spirit; rather, the RCC dispensed its own perversion of salvation through the giving or denial of sacraments, and forcing conversion by the sword.

It was not until The Renaissance, when students learned Greek and studied the New Testament in its original language, that scholars began questioning the RCC. The Inquisition tried to silence such men and women, but eventually a Reformation began which demanded the Bible be taught in its purity so that people could experience the new birth promised within its pages.

Christianity, at least New Testament Christianity, is not a religion of rules, sacraments and traditions. Fundamentally, it is about an intimate, experiential relationship with Jesus Christ, through the imparting of the Holy Spirit, to the one who has trusted their salvation solely to Christ. The evidence that this has taken root is in the convert producing the fruits of the Holy Spirit through a transformed life. If that transformation is not absolutely evident, then it is extremely doubtful that the person has anything other than a new form of religion, rather than a real relationship. The Christian singer and song writer, Keith Green, once said that, 'going to church doesn't make you a Christian any more than going to MacDonald's makes you a hamburger'.

Chapter Thirteen: Islam

The Rise of Islam

According to Warren Hollister in his *Medieval Europe: A Short History;*

In the first hundred years of its existence, Islam shattered the Christian domination of the Mediterranean Basin, destroyed the Persian Empire, seized Byzantium's richest provinces, absorbed Spain, pressed into the heart of France, and expanded far into southern Asia.

Mohammad was born in Mecca in 570AD. His father, a Quraysh of the Hashemite clan, died before his birth and his mother also died before he was six years old. He was unable to have a formal education and was most likely illiterate. Mohammad lived with his uncle. He was from a Bedouin tribal environment and during his teens worked as a camel driver, a job which took him with his merchant uncle to Syria and onto the peninsula to the North. The Hashemite tribe shared the responsibility of the office of the trustee of the Ka'aba (ancient Arab shrine), its idols, its Black Stone, and the nearby sacred well.

There were 360 tribal deities associated with the Ka'aba shrine, a cube-shaped building called 'the house of Allah'. The community in which Mohammad was raised worshiped Allah and his three goddess daughters - Allat, Munat and al-Uzzah.

Many scholars believe that 'Allah' is just a contraction of the personal name of the chief god of the Ka'aba, the moon god. The minarets, shrines, mosques and flags of Islamic countries still bear testimony to this god in their symbols of the crescent moon.

Pre-Islamic Arabs also believed in jinn, Satan, good and evil omens, etc. They were polytheistic people.

In 595AD, at the age of twenty-five, Mohammad married a forty-year-old widow who was his employer and successful merchant. Over the next fifteen or so years he travelled extensively and encountered both Jews and Christians. He is said to have been a deeply religious man, and upon hearing the Trinitarian doctrines of the Christians, believed that they were polytheists, worshipping three gods. The Christian belief of the incarnation was completely rejected by Mohammad, as he believed that God could never become human.

At the age of forty Mohammad began to spend time in isolation, often going to a cave near Mecca. Tradition says that he was seeking God at these times, and trying to understand spiritual questions which bothered him. It is also said that he took fits which may have been epileptic in nature. One night in his cave he had what he described as a vision in which an angel appeared to him and commanded him to recite certain words which are now written in Sura 96 of the Qur'an. He claimed that the angel's name was Gabriel - the same name as the angel who appeared to the Virgin Mary. When he returned to his wife, he told her that he was unsure whether he was possessed by a demon, or insane, but there was no doubt that he was uncertain that his vision was of God.

Some records say that he was not at all distressed about his vision, whilst others say he contemplated suicide. He isolated himself for three years and eventually his wife convinced him that 'Allah' had spoken to him. Mohammad is said to have been taken over at times by a voice not his own and would spontaneously start reciting rhapsodies in Arabic. After a long season of self-doubt, so tradition states, and under the influence of his wife, he became convinced that he was indeed the true prophet (nabi) and apostle (rasul) of Allah who had been given a special mission. This 'Allah' was supposed to be the same god who was known to both the Jews and Christians.

Are Allah and Jehovah the same God?

Consider that the root of the word 'Islam' is 'submission', albeit Muslims would say a voluntary submission to God. The Bible, on the other hand, teaches that the greatest commandment is to 'Love God with all your heart, soul, mind and strength'. Submission can be forced, but love must always be given voluntarily. Islamic history shows that the meaning placed on 'voluntary submission' has always been to voluntarily submit or die.

One might argue that Christianity in the Dark Ages adopted a similar policy of force; however, this must be recognized as in direct opposition to the New Testament emphasis on loving one's enemies and can never be justified within Biblical Scripture. Muslims who force submission on infidels are obeying the fundamental tenants of Islam; Christians who force Christianity onto others are fundamentally disobeying the gospel. Islam and Christianity have blatantly opposing theologies in this regard.

A close examination of Islam's teaching about Allah reveals other facts which make this god completely different to the Bible's revelation. Although the Qur'an teaches that 'God is nearer than a man's jugular vein', there is no way to have an intimate relationship with him as he is 'so far above every man in every way that he is personally unknowable'. Islam also teaches that Allah is the source of both good and evil. He is Al-Hadi, the one who guides, and also Al-Muthill, the one who leads astray. This idea is fundamentally opposed to the Biblical character of God.

In the early days of his mission, Mohammad preached against the social injustices and pagan worship in Meccan society. The leaders of this society were not pleased by this message, but Mohammad's rich uncle Abu Talib, and the considerable wealth he had received from his wife, afforded him protection. Mohammad took the sacred Black Stone to Medina and set it up there, preaching that it could be related back to Abraham.

Both his wife and uncle died in 619 and he lost two of his most ardent supporters; however, he continued to gain a following. After the death of his wife Mohammed married a new wife every year over the next fourteen years, including the divorced wife of his adopted son. After some three years, in 622, Mohammad and his followers went to Yathrib, which is now called 'Medina' from *madinat al-nabi,* which is literally 'City of the Prophet'. This is considered to be the decisive moment of the beginnings of Islam and the year 1 in the calendar used by the Islamic world. After some time Mohammad became both the civil and religious leader of Medina, continuing to win new converts to his religion.

Mohammed hired mercenaries, raised an army and attacked the caravans of Mecca, forcing its surrender in 630. Arab people, like the Romans, believed that the gods fought on the side of the victorious army. When Mohammed's mercenaries defeated Mecca, the people decided to follow "Islam". At the time of his death, in 632, the Meccans and many Arabs outside of the two cities of Mecca and Medina had begun the militant religion of Islam.

The five main obligations of a Muslim:

1. The confession of faith. "There is no god but Allah, and Mohammad is his prophet".
2. Prayer five times a day.
3. Charitable gifts.
4. Fasting in the holy month of Ramadan.
5. Pilgrimage to Mecca.
The word Islam means 'submission to the will of Allah'.

Islamic Writings

The main source of 'divine revelation' is the Qur'an, which is supposedly the words of the prophet Mohammad. Secondly is the Hadith which records the traditions and other words of Mohammad, and thirdly, the Ijma which consists of the 'accord of the faithful', the body of law followed by devout Muslims. Taken together these three represent the 'Sunna', which is translated 'The Path'. The Hadith also claims that Mohammed was pre-existent and the purpose of all creation; indeed, Muslims will turn a deaf ear to criticism of Allah, but any criticism of their prophet is met with vengeance from even liberal believers of Islam.

The Spread of Islam

The initial spread of Islam is recorded over a period of exactly one hundred years dating from Mohammad's death in 632. This was a religion with an ambition to take over the entire world. All idolaters must either accept Islam or be slain by the sword, but Jews and Christians, those who held to monotheist faiths, received a special status, being tolerated on condition that they pay a special tax. The rationale behind this was simply that, in Mohammad's mind, both Jews and Christians shared the same Abrahamic heritage as Muslims, albeit Islam was the latest and most complete revelation from 'Allah', therefore all were worshipping the same god.

The wars between the Roman Catholic Empire and Persians had left both sides exhausted and vulnerable to attack by the new Islamic invaders. In the 620s the Byzantine Empire, led by the Emperor Heraclius, took back Syria, Palestine (including Jerusalem), Egypt and invaded Persia. The cross, which was reported to have been the one on which Christ died, was recaptured from the Persians and deposited back in Jerusalem.

The Muslims, led by 'caliphs' (successors of Muhammad), took Damascus and, in a siege lasting two years, captured Jerusalem, although the cross was taken secretly to Constantinople. The exhausted Byzantine forces were no match for them; the wars with Persia had left Byzantine spread thinly with little money to purchase mercenaries. By 650 Mesopotamia had been conquered, and also parts of Asia Minor and North Africa. The Arabs also developed sea power and took Rhodes, parts of Cyprus, and raided Sicily and Southern Italy. They repeatedly attacked Constantinople in the 670s but were beaten, partly through the use of a new invention known as "Greek fire", which was an explosive incendiary catapulted into the enemy with devastating effects.

In 711 the Arabs crossed the Straits of Gibraltar, and by 715 had taken over the Visigothic rule of Spain. Their advance was halted in 732 by the Franks in the battle of Tours (or Poitiers). The new Empire of Islam soon divided into a series of 'caliphates' based primarily in Mecca, Baghdad, Damascus and Cairo. There followed bitter wars between some of these states concerning arguments about succession.

Note: Apostasy (leaving the Islamic religion) was punishable by death; therefore, conversions to Christianity were rare. People were forced to join Islam or be executed, and if they left Islam they were executed, although many historians believe that forced conversion was rare, if not only for those considered to be polytheistic.

Islam's Doctrine and Self - identity

Islam at the time of its creation was viewed by some as a Christian sect or heresy. This idea came about partly through Mohammad's admission that he had visited Jerusalem and listened to the doctrines of Christians. Mohammed was well informed about the angel Gabriel long before his vision in the cave. In fact, Islam was closer to the doctrines of Orthodox Jews than Christians.

The following are some of the major claims of Islam.

1. The oldest of religions since it claimed to originate in Abraham.
2. The purist of religions to come from Abraham. Abraham was neither Christian nor Jew but of a 'pure faith' submitting to Allah (Muslim). Abraham is said to have set up the Ka'aba stone and established the rites of pilgrimage. Ishmael, Abraham's first son by the servant girl Hagar, is considered to be a prophet.
3. Received the name 'Allah' from the arch-angel Gabriel. What about the Ka'aba 'Allah', the moon god who was worshipped by Mohammed and his tribe. Are we to believe that 'Allah' is a new name?
4. Received visions while having his 'epileptic fits'. These 'fits' only started after his concern about being possessed, and only recurred when giving his 'revelations'.
5. Christ only another prophet, but Mohammad the last prophet. According to Islamic tradition Jesus' crucifixion was not a real death. Christ never died but was taken up to heaven where He waits to return and serve both Allah and the Muslim savoir, the Mahdi.
6. Many regulations for daily life, but rewards in paradise. Pleasures which are denied in this world are given in the next; e.g., Muslim men must not drink alcohol, gamble or fornicate, but in heaven he may drink to excess, gamble, and enjoy 'black-eyed maidens', all of which are mentioned several times in the Qur'an and Hadith as rewards. That which is sin on earth is a reward in heaven? A schizophrenic god?
7. Personal relationship with God is impossible. God is unknowable. If this is the case, no Muslim knows God, even Mohammed.
8. Incarnation is impossible as God cannot demean himself to stoop to humanity. Also, God can never stoop so low as to have a Son. Jesus, then, is just another human being according to Islam. The Bible claims that Jesus is indeed the Son of God, and God the Son. Are Allah and Jehovah the same God with a different name? The answer is a definitive 'no'. Allah has no son.

9. Holy War is essential and warriors dying in these wars receive the greatest pleasures in heaven. The end justifies the means. Killing unarmed infidels, even women and children, is honourable in Allah's eyes.

10. Very simple religion to understand, unlike Christianity's many paradoxes in doctrine.

By the end of the 9th century three distinct groups have emerged. The orthodox position, the largest group, depended solely on the Qur'an and traditional writings. The other two traditions were messianic and mystical concurrently. The messianic taught that there was a continuous flow of revelation by new prophets claiming to be descendants of Fatima, the daughter of Mohammad. The mystical tradition (Sufis) sought for a personal relationship with God, something which was deemed to be utterly impossible by Mohammad.

The Arab cultures thrived so much so that in the tenth and eleventh centuries Arab scholars were the greatest philosophers and scientists of their age. Greek philosophy, including Aristotle who was virtually unknown in Latin Europe before the twelfth century, was translated into Arabic in the eighth century by Greek scholars who belonged to heretical Christian sects. The Arabic world of the Middle Ages was also known for its agricultural wealth and commercial prosperity, and its power resembling the Hellenistic and Roman empires in the size and grandeur of its cities at this time.

Islamic Eschatology (Theology of the Future)

Islamic eschatology is taken from both the Qur'an and Sunna. Both mention Islam's version of Jesus, a Jesus completely removed from the Christ of the New Testament. For Muslims, Jesus was a Muslim before Mohammed. Jesus was just a man, a prophet who was never crucified. He never died, but was taken up to heaven where he waits for Allah to send him back. He will correct all of the false teachings about him by Christians and give Christians an opportunity to accept Islam. He will destroy Christianity and Judaism, establish Sharia Law, and play a key role in the Islamic version of the Day of Judgment in the End Times. Jesus will rule under the authority of the Mahdi for 7 or 40 years (both are taught), will marry, have children and die, but be resurrected on the Day of Judgement.

Islam teaches that there are three signs which herald the Last Days, each one connected to a specific person.

The first is the Mahdi, the Twelfth Imam who is believed to be in hiding at present. His role is to complete the worldwide domination of Islam and Sharia Law. All who refuse to submit will be destroyed. The Madhi's armies will conquer all unbelievers under their banner, a black flag which bears the word 'punishment'. He will begin with the nation of Israel and establish his rule on the temple mount in Jerusalem. He will rule for seven years, do great miracles, bringing wealth and prosperity to all who submit to Allah. He will arrive on a white horse as described in Revelation 6:2, indeed, this passage of the Bible is quoted. The Islamic Mahdi, and the actions he is to fulfil, fit the Bible's description of the coming Antichrist exactly.

The second Islamic sign of the Last Days concerns Islam's version of Jesus. He will act as stated above. The role of the Islamic Jesus is basically identical to the person described in Revelation as the 'false prophet', the one who aids the Antichrist. Fundamentally, this Jesus will claim that he is the real Jesus and command all Christians to reject the traditional Christian Christ and accept him instead. He will worship Allah and order all Christians to do the same or be destroyed. Islamic teachers state that he will 'shatter crosses and slaughter pigs' - symbolic language for the destruction of Christianity and Judaism. He will also destroy the Masih ad-Dajjal, a one-eyed antichrist figure who tries to deceive Muslims.

The Dajjal is the third sign. He arrives on a mule, is blind in one eye, is a false worker of miracles, and an infidel. This person claims to be the Son of God, a divine figure; indeed, he claims to be Jesus Christ. There is a great battle and the Islamic Jesus kills him.

Points to Ponder

1. Like the Mormons, Islam is the product of a so-called angelic revelation to a single individual. In the case of the Mormons, the angel Moroni to Joseph Smith, and for Mohammad, the arch-angel Gabriel whose name he may have found in the Jewish scriptures or Bible. In both of these cases the experiences are not verifiable.

2. Consider that Mohammad was a pagan goddess worshipper and very devout. Consider that he also had 'visions' while he was experiencing 'epileptic fits'. The idea of epileptic fits is a modern way of understanding his experiences for those who are hesitant to say he was manifesting a demonic spirit. By his own testimony he told his wife after his experience, "I don't know whether I am insane or possessed". It was his wife who convinced him that Allah was speaking to him.

3. Many sections of the Qur'an and Sunna are taken from the Hebrew Bible and New Testament, although changed to fit with Islamic teachings. For example, God's name is changed from Jehovah to Allah. The history of the Jews in Egypt, and their liberation through Moses, has been changed to read as though Jews were Muslims. In one passage, which is not in the Bible, Pharaoh tells Moses he's going to cut off his hands and legs and crucify him.

It was around 1300BC when Moses was in Egypt, and crucifixion wasn't invented as a punishment for another 1000 years. Also, there were no Arabs in Egypt as Moses was sent to the Jewish people. Mohammed cannot change this piece of history, so instead he makes the Jews pre-Islamic Muslims.

In the Hebrew Bible the Jews are called God's people, but Mohammed's version calls them 'Moses' people'. Although the fundamental story of Exodus is told in the Qur'an, it has been changed to fit Islamic teachings. Was Mohammed a plagiarist?

4. Jesus Christ is considered by Muslims to be a prophet of Allah, a messenger. He is mentioned many times in the Qur'an as the one who is given the Gospel and knows the Torah. Mohammed also states that Jesus was not crucified, against all the evidence - rather, Jesus ascended into heaven and will return to destroy Christianity and Judaism, and aid the Islamic messiah in establishing Sharia law worldwide. These teachings completely contradict Jesus' teachings and mission. Islam denies the death of Christ in order to deny His Divinity and resurrection.

According to Islamic traditions, their Mahdi will find a new Torah and Gospels which are supposed to be the true ones. These new writings confirm that both Jews and Christians have been entirely wrong about God and Jesus Christ.

Furthermore, the message of Jesus (within the Christian gospels) and Mohammed are almost opposite. Jesus commanded that we 'love our enemies and pray for those who persecute us'. Mohammed orders his followers to 'slay unbelievers'. There are a multitude of contradictions within the Qur'an which show that Mohammed, although knowing something of the Bible's teachings, hadn't done his research well enough.

5. The Qur'an and Sunna use exact details of the Bible, especially the Book of Revelation, and portray a sequence of End Time events which are exactly opposite to Christian teaching. Revelation states that the Antichrist will ride a white horse and be aided by a false prophet who claims to be Jesus Christ. Then Christ Himself will appear and destroy both of them. Keep in mind that Jesus warned that in the Last Days false prophets would appear claiming to be Him and deceiving people through miraculous signs.

For Further Reading
Cantor, Norman. *The Civilization of the Middle Ages.*
Hollister, C Warren. *Medieval Europe: A Short History.*

Chapter Fourteen: Gnosticism, Kabbalism

Gnosticism and Kabbalism both began at around the same time, one from Judaism and the other Christianity. They have a great deal in common, especially the idea that secret truths are hidden in the Hebrew Bible and the teachings of Jesus.

Gnosticism

The Book of Acts, chapter 8, records the meeting of Simon Peter, an apostle of Christ, and Simon Magus who was considered to be a sorcerer. After seeing that people received the Holy Spirit after the apostles laid hands upon them, Magus tried to purchase this power with money. Simon Magus had taken an interest in Christian theology but was never converted. According to tradition, he became the father of Gnosticism, a cult which was considered a heretical form of Christianity. Keep in mind that Simon Magus was a Samaritan by birth. His mother was a Jewess and father Persian. There was a great deal of animosity between Jew and Samaritan, and perhaps this led Simon to seek other answers to life rather than within the pages of his mother's religion of Judaism.

Gnostic Teachings

Gnosticism comes from the word 'gnosis', or knowledge, and in this case, a secret knowledge available to only a select group. Gnostics believed that there was an uncreated god/goddess who created several Aeons, one known as Sophia (Greek for wisdom). Sophia, in turn, created demigods. One of the demigods was the Hebrew God Jehovah. According to the Gnostics, Jehovah created the universe and all material things, but, because he was a jealous god, he was responsible for evil in the world. Jehovah tried to stop the first humans from receiving knowledge. After they tried to gain it by eating of the 'Tree of the Knowledge of Good and Evil', Jehovah banned them from the Garden of Eden and punished them. Lucifer is the good guy in

Gnostic teaching; he had crept into the garden to help the humans find gnosis (knowledge) and was then cursed by Jehovah.

Sophia sent Lucifer's brother, Jesus, to teach people how to get back to the truth, but His disciples misunderstood Him. Gnostics believed that the entire material world was evil because it had been created by a lesser god, Jehovah. Therefore, they claimed that Jesus never had a real human body at all; He simply appeared to be human. This particular idea is called 'Docetism', from the word 'doce', 'to appear'. For Christians, this theology, apart from being offensive, reduced the gospel message to a farce. Moreover, if Jesus wasn't a real person, then His sacrifice on the cross was not real, and therefore, ineffective. In his first letter to the Church the apostle John writes against Gnosticism, putting an emphasis on the real humanity of Jesus.

For Gnostics, only the spirit world can be pure and holy, taking its roots back to Sophia who has no material form. For the leaders of Gnosticism, such as Simon Magus, the power to perform the supernatural was given to those who climbed up through various stages of esoteric teaching, and was closely tied to visitations of angels and other spiritual beings.

Gnostic Practices

Little is known about Gnostic practices as much of their literature was destroyed. However, some of the 'gospels' written by Gnostics to counter the Christian gospels still survive, and also a lot of literature written by Christians about their practices. Salvation for Gnostics is to find the spark of the divine Sophia which remains within, and develop it through various techniques including meditation and asceticism. Many scholars have seen a very direct link to Eastern religions here, especially some of the early teachings in the Gathas and Avestas, the writings of the Zoroastrians. This would not be unlikely as Simon Magus' father was Persian and may have had access to such literature.

Women played a large role in leadership, especially because of their communication with spirits and angels who presumably passed on secret information about salvation, not unlike what we have seen in shamanism. Within Gnosticism there is a great emphasis on the human person as divine, and self development to full divinity as in Hinduism and Buddhism. Self is essentially good because humans can become divine, and many Gnostic practices resemble closely the religions of the Aryans.

From the writings which have survived, it appears that Gnosticism split into two radically different factions. On the one side were the ascetics who taught that the body must be overcome and restrained. Strict forms of self-discipline were applied in order to gain higher spiritual awareness.

On the other side was almost the complete opposite. Some Gnostics believed that the body could not affect the spirit at all and practiced extremely liberal forms of sexuality, indulging in orgies. They believed that the emotions, lusts and desires must be released in order to free the spirit from bodily bondage, in a similar way to the people of the past who had worshipped Baal, Ashtorah, etc. In general terms, anything that Jehovah banned must be the way to spiritual freedom. Jehovah had destroyed the cities of Sodom and Gomorrah for their immoral sexuality and homosexuality, so it was assumed that similar practices must be beneficial in finding secret knowledge.

Kabbalism

Kabbalism has been around for about 2000 years, although some scholars believe that its roots began while the Jews were prisoners during the Babylonian Exile in the 6th century BC, citing the many similarities between Zoroastrianism from the Aryans. It can be defined as a theosophical (mystical) approach to understanding or experiencing the Hebrew Bible, which began to be taught in secret about 100 years before the birth of Christ with the 'Works of Heaven' and 'Divine Chariots', written by Rabbis around this time. According to Kabbalist tradition, the secrets of Kabbalism were handed down and then finally compiled in the *Zohar* in the 11th to 13th centuries AD.

The idea of Kabbalism is that behind the stories of the Hebrew Bible is a mystical, secret truth which is known only to a select few who pass it on to others. Stories such as the Tree of Life, Moses speaking to God through the burning bush, Ezekiel's flying chariot, Jacob's ladder that extended to heaven, and others, have a secret meaning.

Like Gnosticism, Kabbalism has the idea of a god who is unknowable, an uncreated being behind everything else. This god is called Ein Sof, the 'Infinite One'. Ein Sof is said to be the one from whom Jehovah came into being. From Ein Sof came what, for Kabbalists, are the Ten Sefirot - emanations of energy which form the Kabalistic Tree of Life. The goal of Kabbalists is to unite these ten energies through self-development, and thus be united with Ein Sof.

Zohar

The Zohar, a word meaning 'splendor' or 'radiance', is found in the Book of Ezekiel and also in Daniel 12:3 which reads; 'the wise ones will shine with the radiance of the firmament'. The Zohar is the most popular of Kabbalist teachings and was first published by Moses de Leon in the 13th Century AD. De Leon ascribed the work to Shimon bar Yochai, a 2nd century mystic who supposedly spent thirteen years in a cave hiding from the Romans and reading the Torah. He is said to have been inspired by the Prophet Elijah to write the Zohar. Many modern scholars believe that it was De Leon himself who wrote the Zohar, attributing it to Yochai in order to give it value financially, but this claim was denied by his closest followers.

Kabbalist Teachings (Generally)

The Zohar contains discussions of God's nature, mythical cosmology (astrology), mystical psychology, the nature of the human soul, the relationship of Ego to Darkness, and the 'True Self' to the 'Light of God'. There are many different branches of Kabbalism and interpretations of beliefs; therefore, we will speak in general terms. Kabbalists believe in two aspects of God.
Firstly, that God in His essence is infinite, utterly transcendent and unknowable. Secondly, God as manifested. God is knowable through various emanations from Him, both spiritually and physically. Humans, as emanations of God, are able to perceive God through the mysteries He has hidden through secret messages in the Torah and other revelations.
Humans can climb a type of spiritual ladder by doing spiritual actions and good deeds. In this way a person becomes righteous and moves along the journey towards perfection. However, the righteous person must be careful and hold everything in balance. An over-emphasis on justice might lead to unfair punishment, excessive love might lead to sexual sin, etc. This in turn can be interpreted as the

origin of evil. Some Kabbalists believe that evil originates from God because evil is thought to be able to exist from an excess of good, while others believe that evil simply must exist as a contrast to good.

Human beings represent both the physical and spiritual aspects of God and are, therefore, the center of the creation and universe as manifestations of God. The human soul has three parts or levels of being - from the most base animal part linked to cravings and instinct, to the highest 'super-soul' which makes humans distinct from all other creatures by virtue of our ability to communicate with God.

Reincarnation is a common belief in Kabbalism, and one which has been controversial. Some Medieval Jewish Kabbalists insisted that only Jews have the pure souls which can reincarnate into the highest echelons of the divine - an interpretation of the Jews as God's chosen people. All other humans (Gentiles) have only a base soul, but these can be reincarnated as Jews in order to continue their spiritual journey. This teaching caused a great deal of tension and was dropped by many later Kabbalist teachers.

Modern Kabbalism

Over the last 200 years Kabbalism has changed from an almost exclusively Jewish religious form to a universal religion in its own right. Its teachings have also taken root in occultism, the Masonic Lodge, New Age Movements, Golden Dawn and the likes. Some of these groups, such as Golden Dawn, are associated with forms of magic and connection with spirits through Tarot, Astrology, spirit channeling, and the worship of angelic beings. New Age societies which practice Kundalini Yoga and meditation, use Kabbalism as it relates to Hindu and Buddhist traditions, whilst Hermetic Kabbalism is tied to alchemy, spirit guides, and so forth. Famous occultists such as Alistair Crowley, the angelic magic of John Dee, and philosophers such as Hegel and Karl Marx, all practiced Kabbalism in different forms.

In general terms, modern Kabbalism teaches that the Divine Light can be found in every human being. As emanations from 'god', we *are* god and therefore divine in our own right. Our role is to re-create ourselves in absolute divinity through various means. Human beings, as emanations of the cosmos, are the center of the cosmos. Without humanity, God would have no manifestation.

Points to Ponder

In a world in which it is often difficult to find answers to difficult questions, it's not difficult to imagine why mystery religions flourish. People love mystery and magic. Books like the Harry Potter series are good examples of our fascination to be more than what we are, to have magical powers and know the mysteries of life.

Gnosticism and Kabbalism appeal to such people, as they appeal to a basic instinct within us that there is more to life than meets the eye. Human beings have an instinct or intuition which calls us higher, which quietly whispers the idea that we were created for perfection. Science claims that we use less than 15% of our brain potential, adding fuel to the fire about what we could achieve if we developed ourselves. But how do we do it?

Many people are simply not satisfied to recognize teachings about the debilitating effects of sin, such as is taught in the Bible. Like Eve, we want it all now, we want answers now! Gnosticism and Kabbalism both promise answers to the select few who dedicate their lives to occult pursuits, and both lead people towards beings who are not natural to this world. There's nothing new about that, but it should ring alarm bells. If the only way human beings can really manifest what we consider 'supernatural' phenomena is through joining to 'spiritual beings', then why has our Creator limited us? If we could use the other 85%, without assistance from otherworldly creatures, would we be 'supernatural' ourselves?

Perhaps the problem lies in recognizing the dark side of our natures which manifests itself every day throughout the world. One only needs to watch the news for thirty minutes to see what humanity is capable of in terms of evil, and this with just 15% of our brain potential. Perhaps God would see our natures corrected before we are given power.

Both Gnosticism and Kabbalism are grounded in the idea that God has hidden knowledge from us. For Gnostics, this is because God is evil and jealous; for Kabbalists, the journey through mysticism is supposed to test our natures along the way. Both of these religions have their roots in perverted interpretations of the Bible, yet millions who have taken the Bible's instructions on face value have discovered that mystical experience Christ called being 'born again' and seen their characters transformed. For such people, the key was in recognizing their potential for evil and their real love of 'sin'. That word sin is almost exclusive to the Bible, a word people don't like to hear as it attacks our pride and sense of autonomy.

For the Gnostic and Kabbalist, knowledge must be given *now*, whether God wills it or not. For those who interpret the Bible from the view that God wanted us to understand it without a PHD in mysticism, knowledge will be given as God wills, in His time. The Gnostic wants it all now, in this lifetime; the Christian is willing to trust in the benevolent God to develop us in *His* time.

Chapter Fifteen: Mormonism

At the end of the eighteenth century a great Christian revival broke out which spread across parts of Europe, especially Great Britain, and to North America. This was a traditionally Bible-based revival known as the Great Awakening and was attributed to the work of the Holy Spirit. Within fifty years of this, several groups of pseudo Christian religions sprang up in America - religions which Bible-based Christians consider cults, and even a demonic reaction to the Great Awakening. The first of these groups came to be known as Mormonism and was founded in the 1820s by Joseph Smith.

Mormon Beginnings

Joseph Smith was said to be a member of the Masonic Lodge, an organization with close ties to Kabbalism. He claimed to have received a vision in which an angel named Moroni told him where he could find Golden Plates which were supposedly a chronicle of the indigenous people of America, a group of Israelites who believed in Christ hundreds of years before His birth. Over three months, Smith is said to have dictated a 584-page book which he claimed he translated from an ancient language he had been able to understand through a gift from God. Other sources claim that he had a magical pair of spectacles, glasses which enabled him to read these golden plates. From 1829, Smith, and his close associate, Oliver Cowdery, began baptizing people into a new Church called the Church of Christ.

Later, Smith claimed that in 1820 he had seen another vision of God and Jesus Christ together, and in answer to his prayer, was told he should join no Church as they were all teaching false doctrines. By 1830, he claimed that God had chosen him to be the prophet of the Restored Church, and that the book of Mormon would be the foundational document for this church.

Smith's claims were not well met and, to avoid conflict, he tried to establish what he referred to as The New Jerusalem in Jackson County,

Missouri. By this time the Mormons were calling themselves the Church of Jesus Christ of Latter Day Saints (LDS), and from 1830 onwards were practicing polygamy as instructed by Smith. By the 1850s about 30% of Mormons practiced polygamy openly, and no doubt this was one of the most controversial practices which led to their confrontation with both the government and local organizations. LDS were expelled from Missouri and settled in Illinois for several years, but conflicts there saw the death of Smith in 1844. It is claimed that prior to his death by an angry mob, he called out a secret code of the Masonic Lodge in the hope that fellow masons would save him.

Brigham Young was accepted as the new prophet/leader of the LDS and led his followers to the Utah Territory. In Utah, plural marriage was practiced openly, which led to the United States Congress outlawing the practice. In 1890 the LDS officially announced the end of plural marriage; however, such multiple unions have continued secretly amongst fundamentalist Mormons to the present time.

Mormon Teachings

1. Pre-existence. As in Plato's philosophy, Mormons believe in the pre-existence of all persons as souls/spirits or intellects. This is an interesting contradiction in that one of Mormonism's earliest criticisms of Protestantism is that parts of the Bible were corrupted by Greek Philosophy. Pre-existence means that humans, and angels such as Satan, were all spirit beings before God created the world. Plato taught that the Ultimate God, the Logos, was immortal, and that the human soul was a tiny part of the Logos. Mormons believe that we are spirit children of God and, therefore, of the same essence of God.

2. God as a Man. The God called Jehovah was once a man with an Immortal Father. His origins are described in another Smith translation, *The Book of Abraham,* which is supposed to be a text written upon Egyptian papyrus which Joseph Smith translated. In this book, God is said to dwell on a planet/star called Kolob, the 'Throne of God'. He has a tangible body like ours. Due to his good character, Jehovah ascended to being a great god with his own planet (Kolob) and then proceeded to create our universe which he rules. Human beings are also capable of achieving god status, of having their own

planets and producing spirit children, depending entirely on their lives on earth.

3. Human life on earth is merely a testing ground to determine each spirit's future. Freedom to choose means that most will make mistakes and sin; however, through good works one can earn their way upwards to the highest of three different levels of heaven, a doctrine recorded in Smith's work, *Doctrines and Covenants*.

4. Jesus Christ is the naturally conceived son of Jehovah and Mary. God, in his physical body, had sexual relations with Mary to produce Jesus.

5. Jesus is able to offer atonement for sins. This is not a 'salvation by grace' theology, but rather an opportunity for the person to get back on track on their spiritual journey towards ascension. Jesus is therefore more of an exemplar - an example to follow in order to gain a higher ascension.

6. Forgiveness of sins is tied to compliance of Mormon Laws and Ordinances. The Book of Mormon has greater authority than the Bible; in fact, the Bible is considered to have been changed, or parts of it lost - supposedly the parts which would support Mormon theology.

7. Jesus is the first spirit born in Jehovah's universe, but there are many universes, and other gods rule them as Jehovah rules ours.

8. There is no 'salvation' outside of Mormonism. Satan devised the doctrine of Salvation by Grace alone in Jesus Christ. A person must earn their salvation through good works. However, there are many degrees of salvation and hell. There are several lower realms including 'outer darkness' where the worst sinners are sent, but Smith also indicated that for those living in the two lower 'heavens', after seeing the highest heaven, their existence will be a form of hell.

9. As in Freemasonry, in order to ascend to the highest heavens one must join the priesthood and learn secret rites and handshakes - a spiritual elite who are recognized by Jehovah through the individual learning and application of them. Until the mid 1970's, no black person could become a Mormon priest, and women are banned from this level of Mormon hierarchy.

10. God is married to his goddess wife and produces spirit children. Marriages are eternal for Mormons, whether one has several wives or just one.

11. Mormons baptize the living on behalf of the dead in order to help the dead ascend to a higher level. Mormons also believe that it is

possible to baptize a living person for a dead non-Mormon in order for that person to become a Mormon and, therefore, obtain a higher level of eternal existence. This doctrine would seem to contradict Smith's claim that no one can progress from one spiritual reality to a higher one after death.

12. Ordinances. Mormons have many ordinances, rituals similar in some respects to sacraments, but closer to the idea of a covenant with God. Ordinances include water baptism, ordination into the Melchizidek and Aaronic priesthoods, the laying on of hands, etc.

Mormonism as 'Christian'

Is Mormonism a form of Christianity?

Christianity holds the Bible, both Old and New Testaments, as its fundamental, foundational beliefs, and that the Bible, at least in context, is infallible, inerrant, and revealed by God. The Book of Mormon is the foundational text of Mormons, just as the Qur'an is for Muslims - two religions which both claim angelic revelation and authority by their founders. Any religion must be defined by its foundation; therefore, it would be just as authorative to call Muslims 'Christians', for Muslims also quote the Bible as a secondary source. The Book of Mormon contradicts the Bible in the same way as the Qur'an. Mormons also recognize other books as Scripture, including *Doctrines and Covenants,* and *The Pearl of Great Price.*

Christianity has creeds which are accepted by all Christian denominations. The 'Apostolic Creeds' include doctrines which are absolutely non-negotiable for Christians which include the following:

1. God is Triune in nature. The Father, Son and Holy Spirit are three persons of the Godhead, indivisible and yet individual. Mormonism rejects this doctrine wholesale.

2. Christology. Jesus Christ is the Logos, the second person of the Trinity. He is the physical manifestation of God, the Creator, and the one who was born of the Holy Spirit and seed of Mary, the virgin who conceived. Jesus Christ is both fully God and fully man. Jesus Christ, through His death and resurrection, atones for all sin. Mormons reject traditional Bible-based Christology.

3. The Nature of God. God alone is immortal (1st Timothy 6:16). God alone is the infinite uncreated being. Mormons teach that Jehovah was a man before becoming God; that he married and produced 'spirit children'. This idea is utterly rejected in Christian theology.

4. Satan was created as an arch angel, not a 'spirit being' or brother to Jesus. Such an idea is abhorrent to Christian ears.

5. Salvation is by grace and through faith. Salvation cannot be earned as in Mormonism.

Mormonism is absolutely opposed to traditional Christianity in its beliefs and practices. For the Christian, salvation is by grace, through faith in the saving power of Jesus Christ, 'apart from good deeds' (Ephesians 2:8); therefore, salvation is a gift from God to all those who seek immortality through trusting their lives to Christ (Romans 2: 7). For Mormons, Christ is merely an exemplar. Mormons must, as Buddha stated, 'work out their own salvation with diligence', observing strict rules and entering into covenants, of which many are closely related to The Masonic Lodge.

Joseph Smith introduced many Masonic ideas and practices into Mormonism and remained a Freemason until his death. Masons practice a ritual in which the initiate must wear torn and ragged clothes and get into a coffin, symbolizing death to their former Masonic life. According to the testimony of ex-Mormons, Mormon initiates are subjected to similar rites. Symbols such as the square and compass are taken from freemasonry, as are many of the rites. For example, freemasons use secret handshakes in order to identify other masons, whereas Mormons learn secret handshakes in order to be identified by specific angels and be allowed to enter the highest realms of their three- leveled heaven.

For the Christian, Scripture is a closed revelation. No one has the authority to add to the Bible, although both Roman Catholic and Orthodox Christianity consider their traditions to be on an equal status to Scripture. For Mormons, like Hindus, revelation can be continued as in the case of Joseph Smith.

Leo Tolstoy described Mormonism as the 'quintessential American Religion'. Mormons believe that the Garden of Eden was in North America, that Christ visited America, that the people of the Book of Mormon lived in America prior to the coming of Christ, that the New

Jerusalem would be built in Missouri, and that the revelation for the restored Church was given to Joseph Smith in New York.

Conclusions

If Christianity is a Bible-based religion, in the sense that Christian theology must be tested against the Bible, then Mormonism is definitely not Christian. One may also question the appearance and disappearance of the golden plates containing the Book of Mormon. These plates were supposedly hidden somewhere in New York - not brought down from heaven - but went missing entirely. How could something so important to a religion just get lost or disappear? According to Smith, he returned the plates to the angel Moroni. Whether or not the golden plates ever existed can never be proven or disproved. Stories about the plates vary considerably and, for Mormons, their existence is simply believed.

Chapter Sixteen: Baha'i Faith

Since the introduction of Islam through conquest in the 7th-8th centuries, there have been few new religions to appear in Muslim-dominated countries. The reason for that is simply that the penalty for apostasy from Islam is a sentence of death. Different branches and forms of Islam have sprung up in the Muslim world causing violent conflicts, and today over fifty different interpretations of Islam exist. According to Shi'a Islam, the Mahdi (Islamic messiah) will be the Twelfth Imam who will appear just before the Day of Judgment, rid the world of evil, and establish his kingdom. This Imam was supposed to have arrived in 874 and gone into hiding until the proper time. In the meantime, his message would be given to the people through mediators called 'Babs', a word meaning 'gate'.

In 1844, the Shaykhis, a sect of Shi'a, were convinced that the Bab was about to appear and went in search of him in the city of Shiraz in Iran. Alí Muhammad Shirazi met Mulla Husayn who represented the Shaykhis and convinced him that he was the Promised One - the long awaited Bab, a messenger of God. After a period of time the Bab confessed that he was more than just the 'gate', but rather the Mahdi himself, the messiah of Islam. This messianic claim was the thing which brought him into direct conflict with Islamic government authorities and led to his death in 1850 by execution.

Ali Muhammad's teachings were, in simple terms, a new interpretation of the Qur'an, taking ideas such as resurrection and the Day of Judgment and symbolizing them. This new form of Islam came to be known as B'abism. In some areas of Qur'anic Law he seems to be advocating a separation from Islam, but in others, his teachings are as strict and intolerant as traditional Islam. Due to intense persecution, and the deaths of thousands of his followers, B'abism went underground for a while until the arrival of a new messenger.

Bahá'u'lláh

Mirza Husayn (1817-1892), who is best known as Bahá'u'lláh, considered himself to be the prophetic fulfillment of B'abism. In several of his writings the Bab had eluded to a Promised One who would establish the kingdom of God on earth, and that the people must follow him. Bahá'u'lláh claimed to be this messenger of God prophesied by the Bab who had arrived to fulfill the eschatological expectations of Islam and Christianity, and is the founder of the Baha'i Faith. Baha'i is as much dedicated to the pursuits of unity and tolerance as Islam is to conflict and conquest. Not surprisingly, then, Bahá'u'lláh's claims of divine revelation brought him into direct conflict with Islam and saw him exiled from Persia (Iran) to the Ottoman states, and eventual imprisonment in Palestine, where he died in 1892. Baha'i authors make much of his lineage, claiming that his ancestry can be traced back to Abraham through his wife Keturah, Zoroaster and Yazdigird III, the last king of the Sassanid Empire.

Of his writings, few have been translated into English. His most famous works are as follows.

1. The Aqdas. The Aqdas is commonly referred to as the 'the Most Holy Book' or 'the Book of Laws', and is said to contain the 'Charter of the future of world civilization'. It contains several themes including the appointment of Bahá'u'lláh's oldest son as his successor, the institution of 'The Universal House of Justice', laws, ordinances, exhortations and instructions on prayer, fasting and miscellaneous subjects.
2. The Iqan (Book of Certitude). Fundamentally, the Iqan deals with the idea of progressive divine revelation. It is in a question/answer form, the questioner being a Muslim. Bahá'u'lláh seeks to prove that each religion contains a partial revelation of God through that religion's messenger, and also, that hidden within the Scriptures of every religion are pointers towards the next, an idea similar to Kabbalism. In this sense, Bahá'u'lláh tries to use the New Testament to point to Islam, the Qur'an to point to the Bab, and the Bab to point to Baha'i.

3. The Hidden Words. In Shi'a Muslim tradition, Fatimah, the daughter of Mohammed, is believed to have been visited by the angel Gabriel and given prophesies about the coming Mahdi which she wrote in a book which, if it ever existed, is now lost. Bahá'u'lláh claimed that he was the one of whom Fatimah wrote. *The Hidden Words* are written in such a way as to be a conversation between the reader and God. Both are in the first person, and the reader is extolled to live a life in love with God, who uses terms which appear to have been taken from both the Old and New Testaments, such as calling the faithful worshipper his 'Beloved' (OT) and 'Bride' (NT).

4. The Gleanings. The Gleanings are a selection of the most important of Bahá'u'lláh's works. Subjects, which we will examine later, include The Day of God, Manifestation of God, Immortality of the Soul, The (new) World Order, duties of individuals, and the spiritual meaning of life.

5. Gems of Divine Mystery. In this book Bahá'u'lláh claims that he alone knows the true meaning of the Bible and Qur'an. He quotes many verses from the Qur'an, and a few from the New Testament, and tries to convince his audience that both Jesus and Mohammed were teaching the same message. He quotes the Book of Hebrews about the Word of God being a 'two-edged sword' and translates this as Jesus predicting the Qur'an and rightness of Islam in the killing of infidels. Nowhere does he attempt to translate the many verses where Jesus spoke of Himself as the only 'Way, Truth and Life', or the many false prophets who would follow Him.

`Abdu'l-Bahá

`Abdu'l-Bahá, Bahá'u'lláh's son and successor, took over the leadership of the Baha'i faith after his father's death. In the early 20th century he embarked on a tour of Europe in which he gave several talks which, along with his written teachings (some earlier), give us more insight into Baha'i ideas.

A. The Secret of Divine Civilization (1875). This book was written anonymously by `Abdu'l-Bahá and addressed to the people of Iran (Persia), calling on them to stop spending their days "like barbarians in the depths of ignorance and abomination". He wants to see Iran transformed into a modern nation which has moved on from the restraints of their wrong interpretation of the Qur'an. He goes on to give a brief history lesson, reminding the Iranian people of the height of Iranian culture in the past whilst Europe and America lived in the 'Dark Ages' until the 15th century, the turning point. However, now it is Iran who is behind whilst Europe and America are the leaders in law, order, government and advanced civilization.

B. The Paris Talks. In *The Paris Talks,* given during his European tour, `Abdu'l-Bahá covers a variety of topics. It is within these talks that we are given a greater insight into modern Baha'i teachings.

The following are a summary.

1. Showing kindness and sympathy towards strangers and foreigners through right action.

2. Unity between the peoples of East and West.

In this section `Abdu'l-Bahá suggests that the West is greater in material wealth than the East, but poorer spiritually. He suggests a unity and exchange of wealth and spirituality so that there will be equality between nations.

3. God cannot be comprehended. `Abdu'l-Bahá teaches that, although man is made in God's image and can have a limited intellectual understanding of Him, God cannot be comprehended. He suggests that a mineral cannot understand the growth of the tree, but contributes towards the tree. In the same way, Jesus said 'He who has seen me has seen the Father'. Jesus, he suggests, is a manifestation of God in the same way as any other human being, but not an incarnation, for the Divine can never come down and be the mirror/image, just as the sun cannot descend from the sky. In real terms, `Abdu'l-Bahá states that Jesus Christ is not God the Son; indeed, he rejected the Incarnation and Trinity completely. These teachings are almost identical to Islam on this subject.

4. A call to live in peace and love. One of the foundational teachings of Baha'i is the unity of all humanity. The Baha'i faith calls all nations to lay down arms and join together in peace, thus bringing the dawn of a New Age of God's Kingdom. `Abdu'l-Bahá suggests that 'Holy Spirit' is simply the 'Spirit of Love' which dwells in all men if we love one another. For `Abdu'l-Bahá, people only need to desire to love and this love will be manifested. Like his father before him, he completely neglects the teaching throughout the Bible of the fall of humanity into sin, or the Bible's explanation for war, hatred, murder and similar evils. The Bible is adamant that the image of God in man has been completely tainted by the sin nature which is inherited from

Adam and Eve. `Abdu'l-Bahá never mentions sin, except as an absence of knowledge, or this predominant theme in Biblical Scripture, and therefore, has no definitive answer as to why people turn to war, hatred and racism.

5. God's greatest gift to man. Here, `Abdu'l-Bahá claims that God's greatest gift to humanity is his intellect. It is merely by an act of the will and the desire to love that the New World Order of God's Kingdom will come about. Within the Paris talks, as opposed to the book published in Iran, `Abdu'l-Bahá continually quotes verses from the gospels, such as 'love your neighbor' rather than quoting the Qur'an which he claims is a more recent manifestation of truth. Perhaps he understood clearly that European ears would have rejected his message had he been trying to convince the West that Islam is a religion of peace.

6. The Divine Christ (The Clouds that Obscure the Sun, October 27, 1911). In what seems to be a contradiction to his former talks, `Abdu'l-Bahá claims that Jesus is Divine, the Son of Mary and the Holy Spirit. He says that Jesus' body was of Mary but His spirit of God. This is not the same as saying that Christ is God, but rather a manifestation of God - a man empowered as a messenger of the Divine with a divine spirit.

7. Religious Prejudice (October 27, 1911). In this section `Abdu'l-Bahá claims that Mohammed "taught the people that idol worship was wrong, but that they should reverence Christ, Moses and the Prophets". He says that Muslims and Christians have been at war for 1300 years and "with very little effort their differences and disputes could be overcome and peace and harmony could exist between them and the world could be at rest!" It could be argued that a great deal of effort has been made over the past 1500 years to overcome their difficulties and disputes, but with little being accomplished.

He also says that Mohammed ordered his followers to believe in Jesus Christ and the prophets. To those Muslims who believe that the role of Islam is to bring all nations under Islamic Law and into submission to Allah, perhaps he would suggest that they have misunderstood Mohammed. One of the fundamental tenants of the Baha'i faith is the unity of religions, a One World Religion in which all people recognize one God.

8. The Holy Spirit as Mediator. `Abdu'l-Bahá taught that the Holy Spirit is the mediator between God and man. God Himself cannot

descend to man, but The Holy Spirit acts as a mediator. He uses the sun as an analogy. The sun cannot descend to earth or the earth ascend to the sun; therefore, the sun's rays are like the Holy Spirit between man and God. He goes on to mention the Apostles Peter and John in this section, yet both of these wrote that Jesus Christ alone is the mediator between God and humanity, and that the Holy Spirit is only gifted to those who have faith in Christ alone for salvation - a gift of grace, not of the will, intellect or good works.

9. The Two Natures of Humanity. For `Abdu'l-Bahá, man has a material nature and a spiritual nature. He quotes the 'saints' of Christianity as those "men who have freed themselves from the world of matter and who have overcome sin." He encourages his listeners to follow their example. In this section he writes of Christ as an example of how we should live, but again, it is supposed that by a mere intellectual decision to change, God will bring about 'sainthood' in the individual.

10. The Immortality of Man. "As to the soul of man after death, it remains in the degree of purity to which it has evolved during life in the physical body, and after it is freed from the body it remains plunged in the ocean of God's Mercy." Baha'i faith believes in the immortality of the soul, and that after death the soul continues in a form of spiritual evolution towards God. In `Abdu'l-Bahá's words:"From the moment the soul leaves the body and arrives in the Heavenly World, its evolution is spiritual, and that evolution is: The approaching unto God."

There is no idea of hell or judgment in this teaching. This begs the question of why one would bother to try and perfect their soul in this life if it is destined to be perfectly evolved in the next, no matter what effort is applied before death.

11. Six Requirements of Baha'i

1. To show compassion and goodwill to all mankind.
2. To render service to humanity.
3. To endeavor to guide and enlighten those in darkness.
4. To be kind to everyone, and show forth affection to every living soul.
5. To be humble in your attitude towards God, to be constant in prayer to Him, so as to grow daily nearer to God.
6. To be so faithful and sincere in all your actions that every member may be known as embodying the qualities of honesty, love,

faith, kindness, generosity and courage. To be detached from all that is not God, attracted by the Heavenly Breath—a divine soul; so that the world may know that a Baha'i is a perfect being.If a member of the Baha'i faith continues in these he/she will show the world that a "Baha'i is a perfect being."

12. Water and Fire Baptism. In this section `Abdu'l-Bahá quotes Jesus' words that a man must be born of water and spirit in order to be born again. He teaches that Jesus was merely speaking of love and never of water baptism. He never mentions the term 'born again', for he simply cannot understand or explain something he has never experienced. Prior to His explaining the birth from water and spirit, Jesus tells His listener, Nicodemus, that 'unless a man is born again he cannot experience the Kingdom of God' (John 3). Jesus was speaking of physical birth and spiritual rebirth, and this experience is expounded in the later letters of Paul, John, Peter and the other letters of the apostles.

`Abdu'l-Bahá absolutely denies that there is a form of water baptism (which for Christians is only a symbol of rebirth and not re-birth itself) and suggests that Christian priests have completely misunderstood Jesus' words to mean that water baptism saves. It would appear that he had very little understanding of evangelical Christianity, even though he so often quoted the progress of the Western nations *because* of Christianity.

Conclusions

The key word for those who practice Baha'i is 'unity'. There are three core principles which we can briefly outline.

Firstly; the Unity of God.

Baha'i teaches that there is only one God, the source of creation. In this sense, the God of Islam, Judaism, Christianity, even Buddhism and Hinduism are one and the same. The problem is not that there are several gods, but that different religions recognize God and speak of Him in different ways. The proposition that there is only one true God is recognized by many mainline religions; however, it is naive to believe that peoples of differing religions are worshipping the same being. Consider the fact that Baha'i teaches that this God has sent several messengers to represent Him, yet these messengers contradict one another on a fundamental level. There may be similarities, but the differences are often irreconcilable.

`Abdu'l-Bahá remedies these contradictions in two ways. On the one hand he claims to be the only one to understand the true meanings of the messages of say, Moses, Jesus and Mohammed. The contradictions, therefore, come about through wrong interpretation. On the other hand, he simply uses the small parts of the Bible and Qur'an which are compatible with the unity he is trying to prove, and either ignores the rest, or suggests that the Apostles and other interpreters got it wrong.

Are Allah and Jehovah the same God? If their prophets bring completely contradictory messages, we would have to say 'no'. Even the history has to be changed to accommodate unity. The Bible and Roman records claim that Jesus Christ was crucified by Pontius Pilate. Islam claims He never died but ascended into heaven. In this way Islam and Baha'i can reject Christ's resurrection, an event which, if it happened, puts Christ in a unique position as God the Son, not simply a prophet or teacher/messenger.

There is no doubt that Jesus' disciples believed that He was crucified and rose from death; indeed the whole of Christianity stands or falls on His resurrection. Christ did not come to be a messenger or example; He came to destroy the power of sin and death.

Unity of God is a noble idea, for without it there can never be peace in the world, yet neither Christianity nor Islam place unity as their highest goals. For Christians, unity must take second place to truth - verifiable and existential truth. Christ spoke of false prophets and false messiahs, men who would be empowered by demonic forces. Light and darkness cannot be reconciled, no matter how noble that idea may be.

Secondly; the Unity of Religion.

The idea that all religions lead to God is fundamentally flawed. Why? Because it begins from below, from the perspective of humanity, rather than from above, God's perspective. If religions are simply manmade, then we have made God in the image that we desire and, with a little adjusting, we could all agree on the kind of God we want and can accept.

However, if there *is* a true God, and Baha'i, Christianity, Judaism and Islam say that there is, then He must have His own views on this topic. Jesus claimed that no one could come into God's presence except through Him. If Jesus Christ was and is God the Son, an incarnation of God Himself, then *He* rejects the idea that all religions lead to the same place.

Religions can only be united if people dictate who and what God is. If God Himself is allowed to take part in the discussion, then unity will be impossible without conversion to *His* will.

Thirdly; the Unity of Humanity.

The Baha'i faith teaches that all people are equal before God regardless of gender, race, culture or social standing. The New Testament strongly affirms this principle, in as much as the way people stand before God as creations of God. All humanity is made in the image of God and has the potential to be in a right relationship with Him. In this sense, all people are equally precious in God's sight. However, this principle too has flaws, for people do not act the same. The Bible recognizes the fact of humanity's freedom to choose right or wrong actions, and more importantly, that human beings are driven by various emotions and a sin nature which repels unity with God and with one another.

Unity of humanity is a wonderful and noble notion, but in reality there needs to be a fundamental and monumental change in the human heart for unity to have the possibility of success. If a man is at war with himself, he will be at war with his family. If families are at war with one another, there will be war in the nation. And if nations cannot have unity within their boundaries, there can never be peace in the world. Baha'i offers no concrete answers to how to change the human heart.

The Bible says that a spiritual rebirth is required, and that rebirth can only be gifted through faith in Christ. We may try with all our might to become better people, and even achieve a degree of success, but our sin natures, if not transformed, cannot bring peace to us as individuals, let alone as nations. The unity of humanity can only be achieved through the transformation of individual human hearts. We can stand up for equality of the sexes, human rights, justice and the elimination of poverty, but without personal transformation there will still be murder, rape, injustice and greed.

In many ways the Baha'i faith appears to be a reaction against traditional Islamic teachings and Sharia Law. It contains some wonderful ideas which, unfortunately, are beyond the average person to accomplish, let alone the world. Like Buddhism, it relies on the will and desire of the individual to take control of his/her nature and transform it through prayer, to whatever that person perceives God to be. Like the millions who make New Year resolutions, it requires the desire to make self sacrifices for the good of ourselves and others, but sadly, most people's resolutions can never overpower the sin nature which Jesus said must die through a spiritual rebirth so that the individual could be transformed.

Chapter Seventeen: Jehovah's Witnesses

In order to understand why mainline Christian theologians consider the Jehovah's Witnesses to be a cult, we must take a step back into Church History. In the 2nd and 3rd century a theologian by the name of Origen (185-254) had a profound influence on what came to be known as the Arian Controversy. Origen believed that there was a distinction between the full Divinity of the Father and the lesser divinity of the Son Jesus Christ. This belief sparked one of the longest, most important, and most divisive debates of the 4th century Church.

The Arian Controversy

Arius (250-336), who followed Origen's views, believed that any scripture which pointed to Christ being equal to God was only a courtesy title. Christ was a creature like angels and humanity, but the most important and 'divine' of creatures. Passages such as Colossians 1:15, "He is the image of the invisible God, the firstborn over all creation", were used to support this view - the idea that Christ was the Father's firstborn Son. Christ was created to be the Creator, but nonetheless, He was lower than God the Father.

Athanasius, a contemporary of Arius, opposed Arius' view passionately, arguing that the full divinity of Christ was essential for the Christian understanding of salvation (soteriology). This was a time when the nature of Christ was under enormous scrutiny, a time when theologians were trying to understand the Christian faith intellectually. The issue also went to the other extreme. Was Jesus fully human? If He was, then what kind of human nature did He have? Theologians from both Latin and Greek schools of thought wrestled with these questions for many years before a consensus of opinion was formed and the Councils of the Church created creeds which stated the official position.

In regards to the divinity of Christ, the question could be stated in the way that Athanasius argued.

1. Only God can save us.
2. Jesus is the Savior.
3. Jesus must be God in order to save.

Arius argued that Jesus was a created Savior, but Athanasius pointed out that Jesus could only lift humanity up towards God as far as He was Himself. Therefore, if Christ was not God, He could never 'divinize' humanity. In the same way, if Jesus was never fully human, He could never fully redeem humanity, as He could not be a real substitute for fallen man. On the humanity of Jesus, Gregory of Nazianzus rightly stated that "whatever Christ did not 'assume' in His human nature, He also didn't save", meaning, whatever about Jesus Christ was not the same as us, that part could not be saved.

Arius' position on the divinity of Christ was found to be heretical, not simply from an intellectual viewpoint, but, more importantly, from the many biblical passages that clearly state that He is God. Indeed, no matter how difficult or impossible it is to understand, the Bible states that Jesus was absolutely human in every way, and absolutely Divine, equal to and part of the Triune Godhead.

Jehovah's Witnesses' Fundamental Beliefs

Charles Taze Russell was a keen Bible scholar who formed an independent Bible study group in 1870. He adopted the same approach to the divinity of Christ as Arius had 1500 years earlier. There is no indication that Russell was a Greek language scholar, indeed, had he been, he may have discovered the same conclusions which the early Church Fathers had. Like Arius, Russell taught that Jesus was merely a created son, created to be a sacrifice for sin. Russell rejected the doctrine of the Trinity, as do many people who refuse to believe something which cannot be intellectually understood.

Once Trinitarian doctrine is rejected, questions arise about the nature of Christ and the Holy Spirit. Jehovah's Witnesses (JWs) believe that God created the Arch Angel Michael, who is known as the *Logos* ('Word' of John 1:1), and that Michael became Jesus the man. Jesus was not crucified on a Roman Cross but a 'torture stake', according to JWs. Until 1931 JWs used the symbol of a cross on tombstones, but after this date rejected the cross as a pagan symbol.

The Holy Spirit is not a 'person' for JWs, but rather God's 'active force' - the spiritual energy which emanates from God to achieve His purposes. Obviously, the idea of being 'born again', and filled with the Holy Spirit as a person/counselor/teacher is rejected as well. The many Scriptures which speak of the Holy Spirit as a teacher, counselor, comforter, anointer and empowerer are interpreted as Jehovah using His force to do these things.

God must be addressed by His name, Jehovah, an English variant of the Tetragrammaton of the Hebrew Bible, YHWH. Jehovah is not omnipresent (everywhere) but dwells as a spirit person in His own kingdom. A person may have a relationship through prayer and service. Because Jehovah is merciful, He could never have created a hell where there is suffering; therefore, the traditional view of hell is also rejected. Alongside this, the idea of humans having an immortal soul is rejected. Only those who have been faithful as JWs will be resurrected from death; the rest simply stay dead.

JWs claim to believe that the Bible is inerrant and fundamental to their belief system. However, in order for this statement to be even close to accurate, they have created their own translation called The New World Translation (NWT) in an attempt to make the hundreds of verses which contradict their beliefs compatible. The following is a short list of the most problematic verses in Scripture for JW's beliefs, and some of the NWT's wording.

The Person of Jesus

John 1:1 "In the beginning was the Word (Logos), and the Word was with God, and the Word was God". This is the NIV version, yet the original Greek is even more blatant in its word order, stating in the last line "and God was the Word".

The NWT writes "and the Word was a god". This is an impossible translation from the Greek text. For a start, there is no indefinite article (a) in Greek; therefore, you can never translate as "a god". Secondly, the Greek text states emphatically that "God was the Word (Logos)". The NWT has completely contradicted this particular verse in order to make their version of the Logos a lesser god than God Himself.

Consider Jesus' own words in John 10:30, "I and the Father are one". The Pharisees understood Jesus' claim that He was equal to God and wanted to stone Him. The JWs say that Jesus tried to explain away this claim in the next verses, but the text doesn't support this view.

In Hebrews 1:8-9 God calls Jesus God. There is no hint of Jesus being 'a god'. The Greek text uses the word 'theos', the main word for God, and this word is consistent throughout.

Jesus' disciples also struggled with Jesus' divinity in the beginning. For a Jewish man to worship anyone other than Jehovah was to break the commandments concerning idolatry. Throughout His ministry Jesus continually demonstrated His divinity, so much so that His disciples, for example, after seeing Him walking on the water, worshipped Him as God. After His resurrection many of the disciples continued to doubt. Thomas claimed that unless he put his fingers in the holes made by the nails and spear, he simply would not believe. When Jesus stood before him and Thomas saw the wounds, he fell before Jesus and proclaimed, "My Lord and my God" (John 20:28). One of the most powerful arguments for Jesus' full divinity is the testimony of His disciples.

Jehovah's Witnesses also believe that Jesus is Jehovah's only creation and all else was created by Him. Apollyon (Destroyer of Revelation), Michael the Arch Angel, and The Word all refer to Jesus. Jesus did not resurrect in a material, but spiritual body.

Person of the Holy Spirit

The JWs claim that the Holy Spirit is only an 'active force' of Jehovah, a kind of emanated energy with no personality of His own; however, the Bible contradicts this view entirely. In John 14:16-17 Jesus speaks of 'another Counselor' who is 'with' the disciples and will be 'in them'. Jesus was acting as a counselor as He was speaking and He speaks of 'another'. If the Holy Spirit is not a person, then neither was Christ, for He is the 'other'.

In Acts 5:3 Ananias is accused of having 'lied to the Holy Spirit'. Can someone lie to an active force?

In Acts 25:28 we read that the Holy Spirit speaks, not that Jehovah spoke independently with His 'active force'. In Ephesians 4:30 we read that the Holy Spirit can be grieved, a word meaning a person who can feel the emotion of godly grief and disappointment, and in John 14:26 Jesus refers to Him as the one who will teach the disciples and remind them of all that He said.

The Bible speaks of the Holy Spirit as a person who can be blasphemed, grieved, is a Counselor, teacher, and the one who anoints Christians with spiritual gifts. None of the verses which speak of Him can be diluted or changed to suggest that he is an impersonal energy.

The Bible also powerfully implies that those who have not received the Holy Spirit cannot understand His work or the divinity of Christ. If Jehovah's Witnesses deny the experience of being born again and filled with the Holy Spirit, then biblically, they have denied the very experience which could give them the slightest possibility of having a relationship with Jesus Christ and knowing the Holy Spirit as an indwelling presence which makes them children of God, as stated in the book of Galatians.

Apocalyptic and Prophetic

Charles Russell began publishing what is known as the Watchtower magazine back in 1881. Russell was heavily influenced by Nelson Barbour, a man who prophesied that the rapture, an event in which the faithful will be taken up to meet Christ, would happen in April 1878. When the time came and went, Russell split with Barbour, but his enthusiasm for predicting future apocalyptic events was established and continued long after his death by the Governing Body of JW leaders. Watchtower has been justly criticized for the many prophecies it has made which have never eventuated.

Some of the most important are as follows:

1914. Christ's kingdom will rule the earth and the faithful be taken to heaven.
1916. World War 1 will end with Armageddon and the Rapture of the Saints.
1918. God will destroy the Christian churches and Christians in their millions.
1925. Messiah's Kingdom will be established with Jerusalem as its capital. Patriarchs such as Noah, Abraham and the like will resurrect and be made rulers on the earth.

1938. Armageddon is too close for marriage or child bearing.
1941-43. Armageddon is upon us.
1966-67. The End Times are here...again.
1971-89. The end is here and young JWs should not bother to marry.

Satan

Satan is one of the first angels created by Michael (before he became Jesus). Satan rebelled and was cast down to earth in 1914, the time the Last Days began. All human governments are ruled by Satan, even though the Bible commands Christians to obey the governments. JW's refuse to honor certain governmental edicts.

Life after Death

The natural immortality of the soul is not a Biblical idea, but rather comes from the Greek philosopher Plato. JWs reject this doctrine which is held by many traditional churches. However, alongside this, they also reject any Biblical view of hell entirely. Hades and Sheol are merely words meaning 'common grave', and verses about Gehenna are simply ignored as analogies for death. Of those who are saved, there are 144,000 going to heaven and the rest of the Jehovah's Witness faithful will resurrect and live on the earth. During the Tribulation Period, which has past a few times already, some will become JWs and gain resurrection to life. All other people will simply die and rot as any other animal or creature.

Evangelism

JWs are renowned for their door-to-door evangelism. All adult baptized members are required to submit a monthly report on their evangelical activities. Good works are an essential part of JW beliefs about salvation. Salvation is not by grace alone, but must be earned by service to Jehovah. Those JWs who do not submit a report for six months are considered to be inactive and have forfeited their salvation until they repent and become active again.

Other General Beliefs

JWs are expected to have high standards of ethics and morality, and to dress conservatively. Drunkenness, tobacco and gambling are forbidden. Like all cults, there are extremely strict rules which all must adhere to in order to be considered 'active'. Any JW who publicly disputes doctrines taught in Watchtower magazine, or continually disobeys the rules of conduct, may be 'disfellowshipped' - a word meaning to be shunned as wicked. Only family members living within the same house may associate with disfellowshipped JWs.

JWs refuse to have blood transfusions, based on Acts 15: 29, in which Christians are told to abstain from blood. It was common in the Roman world to drink blood as a tonic, and also to eat cooked blood. The blood was almost always collected at Roman temples, dedicated to pagan gods, and then sold in the markets.

Conclusions

The fundamental and non-negotiable doctrines of the Christian faith, such as God as Trinity and the Divinity of Christ, salvation by grace through faith, and being born again through the empowering activity of the Holy Spirit, are all denied by Jehovah's Witnesses. These denials alone separate them from Christianity in any traditional sense of the word.

On top of this, they portray many of the main characteristics of cults such as exclusivity of membership, shunning and excommunication of those who question the Governing Body, exclusivity of salvation, extreme adherence to rules, secondary sources of doctrine including their own translation of the Bible, false prophecies, and compulsory service as missionaries.

Chapter Eighteen: Atheism

Before we can have any fruitful discussion about atheism we need to define what we perceive as 'God'. If I ask a person if they are an atheist, they may reply 'yes'. If I ask them if they believe in some kind of divine energy, or creative intelligence which exists outside of our three-dimensional world, they may also reply 'yes'. On the other hand, a person may claim to be a theist, one who believes in God, yet perceives 'God' as a manifestation of themselves, or a manifestation of the Absolute within creation - that the entire universe is simply 'God'. There are a great number of human ideas about what or who God is, so for our purposes we will give God a Biblical definition arising from what is believed to be what He has revealed of Himself, rather than what people have imagined him/her/it to be.

According to John Blanchard, God is,

"a personal, unique, plural, spiritual, eternally self-existent, transcendent, immanent, omniscient, immutable, holy, loving Being, the Creator and Ruler of the entire universe and the Judge of all mankind" (John Blanchard. *Does God Believe in Atheists*).

Blanchard's definition is a Biblical one; therefore, from a Biblical point of view anyone who rejects this definition is either an atheist or agnostic - someone undecided. The Bible states that there is only one God, that all other 'gods' are either man made idols or created beings such as fallen angels posing as gods. This is not to suggest that people throughout the ages have not sincerely believed in their myriad gods and goddesses, but rather to say that within the Bible we are given the only viable definition of God which is immutable (unchanging).

We have noted the many changes in the Vedas, Upanishads and Bhagavad-Gita, the absence of God in Buddhism and contradictions within the Qur'an, yet the Bible has a consistent message delivered to prophets, kings and teachers who received independent revelations over a long period - men who never met one another and yet never contradict. On top of that is the revelation of Jesus Christ, the only person in human history to claim to be God the Son, to prove His claim through thousands of miracles and, more importantly, His resurrection. On the basis of these facts, we use the Bible's definition of God.

History of Atheism

Throughout the ages, from the very earliest of human civilizations, people held a belief in a 'Great God' or 'Highest God'. As we have seen, especially in the study of the earliest religions going back to the pre-flood era, the idea of monotheism (one God) was prevalent. After the fall, most ancient peoples record being ruled by creatures who claimed to be gods, shifting people's attention away from an invisible Creator to the immediate issue of appeasing those who had power.

After The Flood we have seen elusions to monotheism in the writings of the ancients, but again, the attention of cultures was on the immediate problems which they began to associate with lesser gods - the control of weather, wars, destiny, etc. In this sense, there is a universal decline from monotheism to polytheism towards a belief in the powers of evil spirits, etc. The Aryan races had a predominant effect on religion through their promotion of violent gods, and it is only after God Himself intervened through the life of Abraham and his descendents, that we witness a group of people who return to the original belief in One God.

The writings of Moses can be dated to around 1300BC, and within them we see a clear definition of the One God. The Jews were unique in their beliefs, yet had a continual influence on the peoples with which they had contact. We noted in the later Vedas and Upanishads, after the Aryan's descendents in the Indu Valley began trading, that a belief in the One High God surfaces again. It is highly likely that contact with Judaism contributed to this change, and in fact Judaism's insistence in One True God influenced the Babylonians who took them prisoner, and eventually the Greeks - the men who applied intellect rather than mere superstition to solving the problem of human existence.

The Early Philosophers

The earliest Greek philosophers such as Thales (585 BC) embraced a form of monism, a belief that the entire universe consisted of similar essence or matter. Socrates placed his hope in knowledge rather than a creator, and was accused of being an atheist because he mostly rejected the mythological gods of the Greeks.

Plato (429-347 BC) came closer to a Divine Creator than his predecessors, but not quite. He taught the idea of a 'Demiurge' who created the world from pre-existent matter and conceived a pyramid of spirits and 'daemon/gods', with the most powerful at the top. He also introduced the idea of the immortality of the soul. Immortality means something which cannot be destroyed. Human souls, in Plato's theory, were tiny pieces of the 'Logos' (God) and therefore, like God, they were indestructible.

Aristotle (384-322 BC) was Plato's pupil, a prolific scholar and philosopher who wrote on ethics, logic, zoology, astronomy, botany and other topics. Aristotle's God existed without matter and was, therefore, not subject to change, yet this God remained uninterested in human affairs - detached and cold.

Epicurus (341-270 BC) believed that the world was made up of atoms, indeed, even the human soul was simply a collision of atoms. Epicurus was one of the earliest philosophers to formulate the basic idea of naturalism, a closed system which basically rejects any notion of existence outside of the natural universe. For the naturalist, nothing exists without matter, therefore the Biblical claim of a God who exists outside of the created world as its Creator and Sustainer is rejected absolutely. Epicureanism is often seen as a precursor to modern scientific philosophy in the theory that if something cannot be proven to exist (through the five senses) it should be rejected.

C.S Lewis explains the consequences of such a system when he writes: 'If naturalism were true then all thoughts whatever would be wholly the result of irrational causes. Therefore, all thoughts would be equally worthless. Therefore, naturalism is worthless. If it is true, then we can know no truths. It cuts its own throat.'

Epicurus is also attributed with being a skeptic because of what we regard as the 'Epicurean Paradox' - a seemingly rational way of disproving the existence of God because of the existence of evil:

If God is willing to prevent evil and not able, then he is not all-powerful.
If he is able to prevent evil and not willing, then he is not all-loving, but malevolent.
If he is both able and willing, then why is there evil in the world?
If he is neither able nor willing to prevent evil, then why call him God?

The Epicurean Paradox may seem, at least on the surface, to be a reasonable argument, yet it fails to consider several important issues. It precludes the notion that evil may be something that God has allowed in order to give His creatures the choice to act freely, if only for a time set by Him. The possibility of evil is essential if real choice between acts of good and evil, which are judged by God, be realized. One may argue that God is ultimately responsible for evil by allowing it; however, evil as a temporal thing may be essential in teaching people the difference between a God who chooses to be absolutely holy, and human beings who, having tasted their potential for evil, reject evil in order to be like God.

Pantheism and Panentheism

Pantheism is the idea that the universe/world is God - the trees, lakes, rivers, mountains, roads and shoe shops. Pantheism was first perceived way back in the 2nd century after Christ with what we now call neo-Platonism. Pantheism is a closed system in which we might say that 'God' invents and then reinvents itself through manifesting into various forms. Even in ancient religions this idea was in seed form. The Egyptians divinized the Nile River, the Europeans the Rhine, and so on. Today we have 'Gaia' mythology which is a feminized form of pantheism. 'Mother Nature', 'Mother earth' are both key phrases in Gaia thought, as is the idea of nature's energy.

Pantheism is simply another form of atheism, a form which has major difficulties in answering the most fundamental of questions. If we are simply parts of a stream of life which manifests and dissipates, how can there be any objective truth? If we are caught up in an endless cycle of manifesting energy, why do we sense that we are individuals; what can we use for a basis of morality; how can we explain evil?

In order to answer some of these questions we have panentheism, which is something of a compromise position between theism and pantheism.

Panentheism holds the same ideas as pantheism with the addition that God is a kind of cosmic energy both within and outside of the system. God in this sense is not eternal, but exists as the force which manifests the world, and the world cannot exist without his/her manifesting powers. Panentheism can suggest that a God/energy also stands outside of creation and that this being/energy has some kind of moral value. Panentheists would argue that Mother Nature punishes us when we destroy the environment - that nature has an identity.

The Renaissance saw the reintroduction of interest in Aristotle's philosophy and sparked the new forms of atheism which have appeared in the past thousand years. Humanism was born at this time - not in particular by atheists, for Roman Catholic scholars such as Erasmus led the charge. Humanism at this time was more about reclaiming the idea of individualism and freedom of thought, especially towards God.

Deism

Onto the scene came the Deists. Deism taught that God was the 'first cause' of everything, but after creation He had basically left the world to work itself out. In this sense, God takes no interest in the world He created and is also impossible to have a personal relationship with.

It seems a ridiculous idea that a God who took the time to create such a universe as ours would then simply abandon it to its own fate. What evidence could suggest such a thing? For the Deist, the evidence was in the lack of evidence for the continued existence of God.

Where was He? Christian theologians, and Christians in general, would easily argue that rather than leaving the world to its own fate, God has revealed Himself in great detail within Scripture, then in the person of Christ, and opened the door to a very powerful and personal experience with Him in which His divine attributes are constantly manifested.

Rationalism and its Allies

Rene Descartes (1596-1650), the French mathematician, is said to be the father of rationalism. Descartes reduced everything through a process of doubt until he came to the conclusion for which he is famous, 'Cogito ergo sum', (I think, therefore I am). Reason and knowledge were to become the new religion of the next period. Descartes laid the foundation for rationality to be the filter through which God must be investigated, although this was never Descartes' intention. The Frenchman thought he'd used reason to prove God's existence, but others saw it another way.

Baruch de Spinoza has been labeled a 'hideous atheist'. Spinoza was a rationalist in that he tried to build a philosophy on reason, a monist in that he believed that there was only one 'Substance', and a pantheist because he taught that God existed only within nature and never outside of it. God, for Spinoza, is neither personal nor conscious, intelligent or purposive; God is what we can see, touch, taste, smell, hear and imagine.

The Enlightenment Period, also known as the Age of Reason of the 18th century, was one of scientific optimism. The Bible was being dissected as a piece of superstitious nonsense which would eventually be discarded and replaced by the new god/goddess Reason. What could not be proven scientifically, rationally, must be thrown out. Therefore, all of that stuff about miracles, resurrections, etc., was no more or less than fairy tales from the ancient past.

John Locke claimed that the senses were the only true way to obtain reason, and then along came David Hume who argued that the only thing our experiences tell us is the fact that we are having experiences. Hume was a skeptic and one of the first philosophers to attack miracles on the basis that they violate the laws of nature. The Age of Reason put humanity dead center and God under our microscope. In a very real sense, we became God and God became the subject of our approval.

The Modern Atheists and their Philosophies

Modern atheism traces itself back to a different figure. Ludwig Feuerbach studied philosophy under Hegel, a philosopher who believed that 'the State is the Divine Idea as it exists on earth', an 'idea'

Marx would grab later on. Feuerbach attacked Protestant Christianity, especially the theology of a man called Friedrich Schleiermacher who insisted that the essence of Christianity was a 'feeling of absolute dependency on God'. Feuerbach turned this idea on its head. For Feuerbach, humanity had created an ideal of perfection outside of itself, projected the desire for perfection onto an imaginary being and called it 'God'. This he termed 'wish projection'.

God, for Feuerbach, was a projection of man's own nature, and for man to reach his destiny God must be taken out of the mind and out of the way. The obvious question that one would want to put to Feuerbach is simply this: "If there is no God, no Creator, then how can destiny exist, for destiny is grounded in the idea of purpose?" Without an intelligent designer existence can have no purpose at all!

Macro-Evolution

Atheism found the perfect partner in the theories of Charles Darwin. In his *Origin of Species,* published in 1859, Darwin provided atheism with an answer to the origin of life, or so it appeared. Evolution theory claims that the universe was created by chance - a random collision of atoms and gases which started a process of life. No Creator, no designer, no purpose; it simply happened. Darwin's theory of Origins has been refuted, challenged and all but thrown out by many leading scientists today, yet it remains, for the only alternative to its atheist conclusions is a God who created the world.

Today, evolutionists cling to the evidence of micro-evolution, of the adaptation of species, a fact that is both accepted by and embraced by Christians, but micro-evolution is and has never been evidence for macro-evolution - the theory of the origin of life. In short, macro-evolution is silenced by its own theories. The Big Bang theory, or as Christians call it, 'Time Zero', or 'In the Beginning' screams the question, 'who started the process? If we know anything at all about science it is this. For every reaction there is an action, for every effect, a cause.

Feuerbach insisted that the idea of God was standing in the way of human progress, of human destiny. This 'brave new world' mentality simply threw God into a basket labeled 'obsolete' and man proclaimed himself his own creator. Not that man had started the process, no - in this system intelligence just happened, the atoms fused into life-forms, the life-forms mutated and, like magic, intelligence appeared. For the philosopher Friedrich Nietzsche, God was no longer needed - He was obsolete - and with jubilation he claimed that 'God is dead'.

Into the mix came Karl Marx (1818-1883), a German of Jewish descent. Marx, like Feuerbach before him, attacked Christianity as a 'pie in the sky' mentality. 'Religion is the poor man's opium' he claimed - a substitute for those who don't have and can't get what they want. Marx saw Christianity as a system which was forcing the poor to submit to the rich. For those countries which were still using a feudal system, this criticism seemed valid.

Once God was taken out of the picture socialism would work, but socialism wasn't Marx's idea. On the contrary, the first socialists were Christians living in the first century - people who considered each other equals; people who sold their possessions and treated one another as a family.

Marx's ideas, or ideals, were put into action through communism. Lenin started the process. Without a God to stand over and judge the proceedings, it seemed logical to simply eradicate any who stood in the way or threatened the cause, such as the intelligentsia; after all, in this system of thought human beings are only complex atomic forms - not sacred in any way. Many were murdered, especially the educated and creative and, of course, those with Christian views and convictions.

After Lenin, Stalin arrived on the scene, a man convinced that he was the 'superman' who was to come, the human messiah that the atheist philosopher Friedrich Nietzsche prophesied would come into the world. On the same continent another man was reading Nietzsche and, like Stalin, was convinced that he was the one. The former became the leader of the communist party, the latter the fuehrer of Germany.

Within the eighty years that atheistic communism ruled in the Soviet Union, 60 million were slaughtered - people who were victims of a regime that used fear as a catalyst for change and death as a punishment for noncompliance.

Existentialism.

The Danish Philosopher Soren Kierkegaard (1813-1855) is regarded as the father of theistic existentialism. Kierkegaard was writing against the dry, traditional, and mostly impersonal Protestant Christianity of his time. For Kierkegaard, faith must be an experience, an intensely personal 'existence', therefore, the term 'existential'.

But existentialism, as it is more commonly understood, is connected to extreme atheism. Atheistic existentialism has little or no sense of humankind, or even society - it is a solely individualistic idea. Every individual must make him/herself what he/she will become, without reference to God. Existentialism, from a social perspective, is a reaction against urbanization, industrialization, and any other thing which tends to destroy individuality and make people a mere cog in the great machine. Such was the teaching of Martin Heidegger (189-1976). Man in the center may seem like a positive ideal, but without God, existentialism heads down a road which has dire consequences.

Jean-Paul Sartre (1905-1980), the French philosopher, was a dramatist, essayist and novelist who used the media to get his message across. He described himself as an atheistic existentialist. He once described an experience where he was sitting in a cafe and felt that another person was staring at him. He claimed that this gave him a feeling of being dehumanized, of reducing him to an object. If God were thus gazing at him, it would make him feel the same. In other words, God's all-seeing eye, for Sartre, made him feel that his self was being diminished, and the only way to make himself feel like a subject, rather than object, was to deny the existence of God.

Once a person becomes aware of himself as an individual, he must determine his own personal identity apart from any religious or social belief. This meant that moral ideas, which are generally based on theistic principles, must be rejected absolutely - otherwise the individual is still submitting to religious ideas. The result of this kind of thinking was summed up by Fyodor Dostoevsky who warned that 'if God does not exist, everything would be permitted'.

The result of Sartre's philosophy was to realize existence itself as completely meaningless; indeed, he claimed that there was 'absolutely no reason for existing'. The universe without God was a cold, uncaring, unfeeling place which existed without purpose or meaning, and humanity was trapped in a void of insignificance. In this philosophy, no human endeavor is any more important than any other - all are equally useless. A half-drunken laborer, picking his teeth with a toothpick, or a violinist picking his strings in the London Symphony

Orchestra, are of equal significance or insignificance - it's just a matter of personal taste.

Yet existentialism had further to go and took the next step through Albert Camus (1913-1960). Camus was strongly influenced by the atheism of Friedrich Nietzsche, but it was his partnership with Sartre which caught popular attention. When their plays, films and books arrived on American shores, their ideas took root. Camus popularized the word 'absurd', a word he used to describe anything in human experience which contradicted the human desire for happiness, purpose and justice. Camus' existentialism led him to the ultimate conclusion of atheism, that 'life is a bad joke' and the only thing left to discuss is suicide. Once God is eliminated from a worldview, the world itself becomes the enemy.

But there is another step in this tragic stroll towards the exaltation of self. We call it 'nihilism'. Nihilism is the logical conclusion of atheistic existentialism and atheism in general. Nihilism claims that 'there is no reason why the universe exists and no goal towards which it is moving; nothing is of real value; human existence is totally meaningless; human beings are biological accidents; there is no life after death and suicide could therefore be a more rational approach than the desire to go on living' (John Blanchard).

Conclusions

We could go on to speak about materialism, an atheistic view that we are nothing more than complex biological machines whose only value is in the minerals that our bodies contain and the gold we may have in our teeth. Determinism is another atheistic view which means that everything we do is determined by what is hereditary and environmental. The world is a closed mechanical thing which is progressing along a path, evolving as it should with no purpose or end. Humans are just a part of the machine and we have no real choice over our actions; we are simply acting instinctively as determined by nature.

If we apply simple logic to atheism it destroys atheism completely. The very fact that atheists, like everybody else, are trying to find some meaning to life, albeit by trying to destroy belief in God, should tell us that human beings have an instinct that we are not just a random collision of atoms. Most of those who claim to be atheists do not live as atheists. We have laws in our societies which reflect moral values.

Where do moral values originate? This question cannot be answered in atheistic terms. Moral values do not exist in the natural world. Yes, there are those things we call natural laws, but these are not moral laws. Animals, insects, fish and birds act on instinct; they are driven by it, and always act within such boundaries. But human beings have the freedom to choose. Our legal systems are set up to provide us with a world where at least a measure of order exists, for without moral laws the world would slide into total chaos.

The other creatures we inhabit this planet with do not need moral laws - something, or someone, gave them moral boundaries which they never cross; they do not have the freedom of choice. No person can live in a society without obeying the moral law which the society dictates; indeed, nobody wants to, even the atheist. Why do human beings understand the need for moral laws? Where do such concepts as love, justice, fair-play, purity, sympathy, compassion and enmity come from?

The Bible's answer to this question is that humans are the only creatures made in God's image. We, like our Creator, are self-aware, and although we exhibit what the Bible calls sinful and rebellious characteristics, part of His image remains. If it didn't, this world would be 'every man for himself' - the very foundation of atheism - and this world would be a thousand times more violent and dark than it is at present. But atheism takes self-awareness and turns it into self-adoration.

Atheists, like all people, are conscious of themselves as individuals. It is self-awareness which separates humanity from all other earthly creatures. This self-awareness makes us ask the profound questions about our existence and purpose - a question that never enters the mind of the rest of creation. However, if we place self in the center and make our individuality the ultimate, and then decide that as individuals we can make our own laws as 'self' determines, what will be the result? Existentialism went down that path, but not completely into chaos, because most reject atheism.

The end result of atheism is a life without reason, a meaningless day to day non-existence which ultimately gives as much value to suicide as to life. Surely, we are not given the ability to create music, poetry, art, love of children and family, the ability to weep with those who weep and laugh with those who laugh, the compassion to reach out to the oppressed and give justice to the wronged - surely we are not given all of this without reason, without purpose.

All rational people seek answers to the big questions because there is a part of us - call it an instinct or reflection of our origin - which calls us upward towards perfection. Even the atheist is trying to find perfection, to find meaning; but when God, the source of our purpose is denied, our purpose ceases to exist.

Chapter Nineteen: New Age Religions

The Age of Reason, or Age of Enlightenment, saw many systems of thought which raised the idea of individuality to god-like status. As we saw in early atheism, once the traditional understanding of God was thrown aside, the veneration of the individual self took God's place. It was during this time that we can find many of the beginnings of the New Age Movement - a movement which is difficult to define because of its diversity of belief and practice. However, New Age ideas can be traced back even further, to the 15th century and the time we refer to as the Protestant Reformation. The ideas which developed over the next few hundred years, and what all New Age religious movements have in common, is self in the center - the idea that the development of self is the development of 'god'.

New Age Religious Beginnings

Philip von Hohenheim (1493-1541, also known as Paracelsus and a contemporary of Martin Luther, was a physician who dabbled in alchemy, the occult, and astrology. He created talismans for curing diseases and connected these to signs of the zodiac. He was also responsible for connecting various elements to parts of the body. Paracelsus' works were closely related to the Hermetic Religion which predated Christianity and practiced astrology, alchemy, and theurgy (connecting with spirits). The ideas of Hermetism are based on the perfection of self through various means including tarot, channeling spirits, the use of chemicals and elements, etc. What started in the 16th century gained pace in The Enlightenment.

Emanuel Swedenborg (1688-1772) is considered by some to be a Christian mystic, but in truth his beliefs are closer to spiritism. He began to experience visions and dreams and claimed to have conversed with spirits from various planets, visited heaven and hell at will, and had conversations with demons. He established what he called the 'New Church', and like the Kabbalists, believed that he had been given a special revelation to translate the Bible purely in spiritual terms.

Franz Mesmer (1734-1815) is identified with what was known as 'animal magnetism' - a term he used to describe a vital force or energy which could be relayed to other people through concentrated mental techniques and the laying on of hands. Mesmer's work lead to forms of 'mesmerism' and hypnosis, but perhaps more importantly for the New Age movement, he was actually acting as a spiritualistic medium and using the powers of spiritual beings to perform healings.

Helena Blavatsky (1831-1891), a Ukrainian woman, was instrumental in forming the Theosophical Society, a group who believe that the 'wisdom of the gods', a secret wisdom, often hidden (occult) and contained within ancient religions, can be learned and practiced. More than any other single individual, her contribution to New Age religion cannot be overestimated. Blavatsky's heritage can be traced back to Russian noblemen and the time of Peter the Great. As a young teen her favorite place was her grandmother's extensive library which contained many works on Medieval Occultism.
At the age of 16 she is said to have undergone an 'inner change' from a lighthearted girl who enjoyed socializing, to a serious student of occult literature. At 16 she also became fascinated with a certain Prince Golitson who was considered to be a magician or soothsayer. Golitson claimed to have connections with a mysterious sage of the East.
Blavatsky wanted independence and entered into a marriage of convenience which she soon escaped, moved to Odessa and, together with a Russian countess Kisileva, traveled over Egypt, Greece and Eastern Europe. This was the first trip of a life of extensive travels in her search for esoteric and occult knowledge. To those who knew her, it seemed that her search was something which drove her; indeed, she felt driven by an unseen spiritual person and was often heard to say 'this work is not mine, but his who sends me'. She also claimed to have seen someone she called her 'Teacher' in dreams - a person she met for the first time in 1851 on her birthday in Hyde Park, London. This Teacher, presumably a Hindu, prophesied that she would spend

several years in Tibet and sent her to India for two years where she received financial support from him.

In her book *From the Caves and Jungles of Hindustan,* about her experiences in India, she recalls meeting a witch. She describes seeing the skeleton of a huge antediluvian creature the size of an elephant, but with four horns, which was used to summon the witch and demons which empowered the woman. The witch appeared out of nowhere and proceeded to perform powerful demonic rites which fascinated her. In her book she speaks of the Aryan people, the ancients who invaded and took over India with the help of giant/human creatures. Blavatsky was certain she had encountered a secluded occult tribe who had in their possession the skull of a god/man, and the witch was possessed by the spirits who empowered this long gone creature.

Blavatsky's travels took her to Tashilhunpo Monastery at Shigatse in Tibet where she studied and practiced Mahayana Buddhism. Her experiences in Tibet are recorded in her work *The Voice of Silence,* a work which depicts her interest in the *Tibetan Book of the Dead.* After more traveling through the Middle East, and another failed marriage, she eventually spent time in Paris and finally settled in the USA where she wrote *The Secret Doctrine* and died in 1891.

The Secret Doctrine

Blavatsky's work entitled the *Secret Doctrine* is foundational in understanding the basis on which all New Age religions are grounded. Blavatsky identifies what she calls 'root races', a term meaning the races from which humans evolved or were originally created. Like many before her, she interprets the Bible through the lens of the Avestas (Aryan/Zoroastrian), Vedas (Aryan/Hindu), Babylonian and Egyptian writings, and claims that great chunks of the original Torah are missing which would bring it into line with these other writings. She rejects the creation story of Genesis in favor of the others. The first races are those which existed before human beings, the fourth is the Atlantis race, made up of semi-gods and giants, and the fifth is that in which humanity is now - the race of the Aryans. This is not the last race, but the entire universe is on a Buddhist-like cycle of evolution towards something unmentioned.

Humanity has descended from these root races which, to the discerning scholar, are none other than the Nephilim - the children of fallen angels and human women. These creatures are mentioned in all of the above literature as 'gods'. Blavatsky speaks about 'seven ancestral spirits' who produce seven Adams or roots of men, that the Tree of Knowledge had seven columns, etc. She believes that the number seven, which she finds predominantly in the Bible, has a secret meaning to understanding spiritual mysteries.

She explains a theory of four continents in the world of which one was reduced to an island and later destroyed - the Island of Atlantis. In order to further prove to any skeptical readers, she quotes the *Secret Book of Dzyan* which, like the Bible, speaks about the giants who ruled before the Great Flood, produced races of giants and men, took human wives, and built huge monuments and cities. But with the coming of the Great Flood, the giant animals (dinosaurs) and giants were destroyed. These creatures were the first 'root races'.

Blavatsky's cosmology is a mixture of all of the ancient texts and signs of the zodiac, Kabbalism and occult literature. Throughout the *Secret Doctrine* she draws from many ancient sources and the writings of theosophist occult literature. By interpreting texts as analogies, especially parts of the Bible, she carefully attempts to show a consistent thread of 'occult truth' in all ancient literature. The genealogies within the Bible, such as Adam and Eve having Cain and Abel, selected writings of the prophets and various isolated verses, are placed in the same categories as the Vedas, Avestas and others.

On the topic of Satan, Blavatsky has much to say, indeed she writes, "But Satan will be shown, in the teaching of the Secret Doctrine, allegorized as Good, and Sacrifice, a God of Wisdom, under different names" (The Secret Doctrine, Vol 2). Like the Gnostics who reject Jehovah for trying to stop Adam and Eve from eating of the Tree of Knowledge, Blavatsky sees Satan as humanity's 'Savior'. In her conclusions she says, "To make the point clear once and for all: that which the clergy of every dogmatic religion - pre-eminently the Christian - points out as Satan, the enemy of God, is in reality, the highest Divine Spirit..."

Where Blavatsky and all other occult writers fall down is in recognizing a principle within Biblical literature which is nowhere present in any other. All ancient texts record their own versions of the past and their present experiences. All of them look backwards. The Bible is absolutely unique in that it records the past only up and until the time of Moses and the Exodus from Egypt. From then on the Bible looks forwards. There is no other ancient text which uses future prophecy to prove its validity. Blavatsky, and others like her, simply ignore this vital fact, for the simple reason that Biblical prophecy refuses to be analogized to fit their agenda.

Alice Bailey (1880-1949) is another who has had a great deal of influence on the development of New Age religion. She was something of a disciple of Blavatsky; however, her occult ideas had a very specific spiritual source. She spent decades linked to a 'person' she initially called 'the Tibetan' and later named Djwal Khul (DK). In fact, her husband testified that she and this person were like 'a joint single projecting mechanism'.

Blavatsky also wrote about Djwal Khul in *The Secret Doctrines.* Understanding Bailey's relationship with DK is essential in interpreting her teachings. Initially she considered herself telepathically linked to her 'Tibetan', but later termed the relationship as 'overshadowing'. In Christian terminology Bailey was possessed. DK is claimed to be a member of the 'Spiritual Hierarchy', and one of 'The Masters of Ancient Wisdom'.

Under the guidance of DK, Bailey founded the Lucifer Publishing Company in the early 1920s, a name that was later changed to the Lucius Trust. This trust became the main publisher of Bailey's works which were given to her by her spiritual guide, and the founding of the Arcane School which trained students in her theosophical views on karma, reincarnation, ancient masters, the divine plan for humanity, and how human beings can achieve their original divine status. Bailey believed that under the guidance of ancient spiritual masters the world was heading towards a New Age called the 'Age of Aquarius' - a new world religion which would be united under the philosophy that all humans are gods.

In order to achieve this end, Bailey founded what is called the 'World Goodwill' organization which promotes the Lucius Trust publication 'The Great Invocation' - a mantra calling on light to enter the minds of men and prepare them for the New Age version of Christ. According to the literature, Christ himself used this invocation in 1945, and all humanity has to do to bring in the Age of Aquarius is to allow ourselves to become aligned to the divine will through the Hierarchy of Spiritual Masters, in the same way that Bailey did with DK. Bailey claims that the 'Great Ones', a hierarchy of spiritual beings, have a definite plan for humanity, which, among other things, means the annihilation of anyone who stands in their way. She praised the era of the atomic bombings of Japan at the end of WW2 as part of that plan.

Modern New Age Movements

Since the 1950s various New Age movements have sprung up until now there is a virtual smorgasbord of groups available to those seeking self-gratification. The 1960s-70s saw the Transcendental Meditation movement of Maharishi Mahesh Yogi, a Hindu teacher who captured the imagination and money of the Beatles through whom the movement gained international fame. Onto the music scene came songs with words claiming 'this is the dawning of the Age of Aquarius' with 'harmony and understanding' - an echo of the Lucius Trust.

The hippie movement, like the Aryans before them, used drugs - not soma, but LSD and cannabis - to get in touch with the 'other side'. The Hare Krishna movement emerged as another blatantly Hindu version of the Unification Church as a Christian sect teaching that all religions lead to God and bliss.

Buddhist, Tibetan and Chinese movements grew as bearded gurus promoted their own particular styles - all with the same message of self-development. Publishers churned out books like *Jonathon Livingstone Seagull* and publications on Tarot, channeling, yoga, using crystals, astral travel, finding your personal spirit guide, and a myriad of other topics including meditation.

In the medical world, alternative holistic medicine - specifically types linked to Eastern religions - became popular. Health and New Age shops popped up throughout the West as the demand for incense, holistic medicines, essential oils, and other items became the latest fad. Meditation centers drew many new 'believers' seeking answers to the emptiness of their capitalistic lives, or a way to deal with stress.

Popular movie and television stars and celebrities such as Shirley McClain and Oprah Winfrey push their own brands of New Age philosophies to millions of viewers worldwide.

Scientology

At a time when evolution theory was rampant, and Christianity ducking its head from a scientific onslaught, onto the stage came a man who became for many a messiah figure, and for others, a fraud of immense proportions.

L. Ron Hubbard, born on March 13, 1911, has had screeds written about him and the religion he founded. Some would disagree with calling the Church of Scientology a religion, but it is exactly that in the true sense of the word, in that it claims to provide people with answers to life, a cause to believe in, and a promise for the future.

Information about Scientology is freely available on public sites such as Wikipedia, so here I will simply summarize as it pertains to our subject. Hubbard's followers have tried to portray him as a 'child prodigy' of sorts - a boy with wealthy relatives who could ride a horse before he could walk and knew exactly what he wanted by the time he was three. Such claims are necessary for an organization that wishes to portray their savior as a Deli Lama figure - reincarnated to give the world the knowledge necessary to save it from destruction.

The truth is that Hubbard was quite an ordinary child and underachiever, although some members of the church will insist that everything negative written about Hubbard is a fabrication of the CIA or other US government organizations. Hubbard was a university dropout and, although his disciples claim he was something of a pioneer in nuclear physics, he actually attained a failed grade in the subject. He had a passion for writing and, in his early years, produced pulp fiction and delved into science fiction.

After some success he produced a manuscript called *Excalibur* - a mystical document which he couldn't sell to publishers even though he claimed it was more significant than the Bible. He also claimed that those who read the manuscript either went insane or committed suicide; such was the power of this revelation. *Excalibur*, according to Scientologists, was then locked away, only to be revealed to the religions' elite after Hubbard's death.

A term in the Navy saw him relieved of command after carrying out gunning practice on an island he thought was uninhabited; the locals didn't appreciate it. After the war, Hubbard declined to return to his wife and children and moved into a mansion with the occultist and 'magician' Alistair Crowley. After participating in sexual occult activities, contacting his 'guardian angel', and sharing Crowley's lover, the two fell out and Hubbard moved on. In 1946 Hubbard committed bigamy when he married a woman called Sara while still married to his children's mother. He eventually divorced the first wife and stayed with the second, living in a mobile home, receiving a veteran's pension, and making money from writing.

He was arrested for petty theft in 1948 and ordered to pay a fine. After a time of depression and suicidal tendencies, he began working on what became the founding document of Scientology - *Dianetics*. This work claims that past experiences are recorded in the reactive mind as 'ingrams' and surface later to cause problems. Through a technique called 'auditing', these ingrams can be dealt with and the person 'cleared' of their effects. Using an 'e-meter', a crude form of lie-detector which measures electrical impulses, questions are asked of the person being audited and responses considered a reaction to previous traumas. Once all traumas have been removed, the person is claimed to be 'clear' - to have an increased IQ and photographic memory.

Scientology offers educational programs which have, no doubt, helped many people who have suffered from under-confidence at school. These programs build the person's self-esteem by helping them identify areas which have held them back. Scientology also offers programs to people addicted to drugs and criminal behavior, and, to all intents and purposes, the religion appears on the surface to be a wholesome organization aiming to improve the planet, and many could testify that the 'church' has improved their lives.

However, when one looks a little deeper, it is pretty obvious that these programs, although possibly well-intentioned, are more likely simply the public face of an organization which has a much more spiritual and egotistical agenda. For the mere beginner, any improvement in their self-esteem which leads to a better life can breed confidence and gratitude, making them ripe for the next levels, provided they have enough money. Getting to the 'clear' stage is expensive if, indeed, anyone ever gets there at all. This process requires specific 'donations', and participants move up through the various levels through auditing - whilst auditing those on the lower levels - along what is called the 'Bridge to Total Freedom' or just 'bridge' in Scientology jargon.

As one goes higher, the cost goes up and the teachings become more and more esoteric. After one becomes 'clear', he/she can begin the OT (operating thetan) levels. One is told that he/she is essentially a 'thetan', a word close to the Platonic idea of a soul. Thetans are immortal and, at some time in the very distant past, we thetans created worlds and universes for our own pleasure.

We were (and can become again) beings of immense power - a power we previously abused and consequently ended up as we are now, trying desperately to get back to where we were before. Sound familiar? We were gods, we are still gods, albeit fallen, but we are basically good and can be as gods again. Hinduism and Buddhism, with a little sci-fi thrown in for good measure - actually, a whole lot more than just a little sci-fi.

What do you do as a cult leader when everyone is supposedly catching up to you in terms of levels of knowledge? Simple! Create higher levels - levels which only you have reached.

Onto the Scientology scene came the 'wall of fire'. Some 75 million years ago, the dictator of a galactic confederacy called Xenu brought billions of people to earth, stacked them around volcanoes, and blasted them with hydrogen bombs. Their souls were then captured and were forced to watch movies which implanted false information into them such as God, the devil, world religions, and anything else which basically contradicts Scientology dogma. These thetans have been adversely affecting humanity ever since, and auditing is necessary to eliminate this traumatic past.

Hubbard claimed that he was the first to discover this secret knowledge, and the first to deal with the 'wall of fire' - coming through the incident with several broken bones. Critics claim that he admitted in a letter to using drugs and alcohol at the time - a claim not difficult to believe. According to Hubbard, Xenu used spaceships which looked exactly like a DC8 aircraft, but without engines; the people wore clothes very similar to westerners at the time of writing, and deployed hydrogen bombs, etc. One would think that a man with such a rich imagination could have come up with something a little more original.

It is difficult to believe that people can be gullible enough to buy into this stuff; however, after one has spent so much it can be even more difficult to get out. By the time of reaching the 'wall of fire' levels, Scientologists have spent tens of thousands of dollars, indeed, sometimes even hundreds of thousands.

Scientology has all the classic ingredients for the desperate seeker of self-development. The initial stages help the self-esteem; the initiate begins to feel he/she is part of an exclusive club and, as time goes by, he learns that he/she is/was a god of almost unlimited power who is changing the world and saving humanity. If you want to deceive people, just massage their egos and dangle a carrot called secret knowledge or mysticism. However, I wonder if far less would get involved if people knew exactly what Scientology teaches before they began.

L. Ron Hubbard. Some consider him as a messiah figure and others as a hypocritical madman. Perhaps a choice is not necessary. Scientology claims to uphold moral values, to honor marriage, to help those caught up in drug addiction and give answers to life. Hubbard's descent into the occult, his adulteress relationship with Crowley's lover, his bigamy, alcohol and drug abuse, testify to a man who practiced 'do as I say, not as I do'.

Scientology could be described as a pseudo-scientific New Age religion. Its fundamental thesis is that of early Hinduism - that Atman (Thetan) and Braham (God) are one. The science fiction aspects are generally kept quiet; in fact, many scientologists may even deny them. Scientology panders to the ego of its participants, has just enough occult mystery to make it a curiosity, and enough social education programs to make it socially acceptable.

Conclusions

To the uninitiated, the idea of extrasensory perception, astral travel, moral relativism, reincarnation, karma, determinism, pyramid power, nature worship, shamanism and the like is very attractive. The mystery/secret factor is always there - the idea that you are more than you realize, and can find your true self, lures many into various New Age religions.

But there is nothing 'new' about New Age religions. All of them have one fundamental philosophy in common - self in the center. To the Christian theologian, their philosophies are as old as the Antediluvian religion and echo Lucifer's words in the Garden of Eden - 'you will be like God'.

For many people on the fringes, New Age philosophy is just a pastime, a hobby, something you dabble in for fun. However, for millions of others it is something far more sinister and existentially linked to demonic forces, such as in the teachings of Blavatsky and Bailey, who, although they taught about the unity of man, also taught intolerance of anyone who dared to stand in the way of their Spiritual Hierarchies' plans for the future of this planet.

The Bible warns that in the Last Days many such religious groups would arise and speak about the return of Christ and claim to be Him, deceiving millions. Many New Age groups promote their own effigy of Jesus Christ in their promotional literature - a Christ completely devoid of any similarities to the one who warned they would claim to be Him.

The most common omission in all New Age religious ideas is that of 'sin'. Sin is not an appropriate word in New Age circles, for human beings are divine, or at least well on their way to becoming so. Like Satan, new agers will, as Satan proclaimed, 'make themselves like the Most High God'; indeed, it is he who leads the charge, he who is the head of the 'ascended masters' and 'spiritual hierarchy', the arch angel who stood over the fallen angels who created the Nephilim, who guided the Aryans with their use of Soma, inspired the Zoroastrians, Babylonians and Kabbalists to seek answers in the zodiac and occult knowledge, and introduced it all in similar forms through his disciples such as Blavatsky, Bailey and Hubbard.

In Biblical Scripture Lucifer is the 'god of this world', the 'prince of the air'. His name means 'Light Bearer' or 'Beautiful One' and he is said to present himself as an 'angel of light' in order to deceive those who refuse to recognize sin. It is no coincidence that Bailey's Lucifer Publishing Company (Lucius Trust) uses his name, or that the Great Invocation speaks about allowing in the light. The Bible also predicts that in the Last Days an Antichrist figure will arise who unites the nations against the Bible's revelation of the real Jesus Christ, and that the world will follow him. The New Age movement believed that this New Age would begin in December 2012, and that their messiah figure will appear soon.

Like the Muslims awaiting their Mahdi to destroy Christianity, New Age adherents wait for the one who will do away with that negative idea of sin and elevate their egos to god-like status. The Antichrist, according to the Bible, has a short-lived reign, for the real Jesus Christ will return to judge those who have followed in his rebellion against God.

Chapter Twenty: Conclusions

Almost every generation has looked up to the stars and asked fundamental questions about human origins, but to the earliest known civilizations the answer to the question of where we came from was universal - a belief in one God who was no longer knowable. For modern minds evolution theory offers the idea that we are just a random collision of atoms and molecules, and as we have seen in our discussion on Atheism, the natural consequence of such a philosophy is nihilism. Evolutionists also suggest that polytheism was the universal belief of ancient civilizations; however, archaeological evidence points to early religious beliefs in monotheism - in one God the Creator.

The idea of polytheism (many gods) can also be found in the earliest writings of ancient religions, and the idea that the Creator is not, or at least no longer, accessible, is unknowable. Over 250 cultures claim that a great flood destroyed all, if not nearly all of humanity, and the gods which they worshipped. In every early religion the focus turns from a transcendent invisible Creator to great beings that walked upon the earth demanding obeisance and sacrifice. According to the Bible, the sin of humanity separated us from our Creator, and the arch angel Lucifer stepped in to fill the void.

Why do all of the earliest religions have so much in common? Why are their stories, their myths and legends so similar? The obvious answer to this is that these stories have been handed down from a single source and retold through the generations. Coupled with these stories are the multitude of examples of early 'art', if art is the right word. It's doubtful that early civilizations were creating drawings for the purpose that art fulfils today, but rather people who had little or no written language were recording events and lifestyles of which they were a part. Ancient drawings are open to interpretation; yet again, I believe that the drawings of ancient civilizations must be interpreted through the writings of people in similar periods and ages.

What does it mean when we see drawings of people paying homage to creatures two to three times their own height? Skeptics of any supernatural phenomenon would say that important people were simply painted larger than the rest; but, when interpreted through the lens of their writings, which speak of their gods as living giants, the drawings come alive and add weight to the writings.

Another important question is why all of these ancient cultures would invent stories and legends about huge living gods who rode in chariots especially built for them, who supervised the construction of massive stone ziggurats, many of which still stand today, and who demanded human sacrifice, taught sorcery, war, astrology and crafts.

If we discount the ancient records of the half god/half human rulers of the ancient world, then why believe anything at all written in their texts? Were they all liars? We have absolute proof that the Aryans invaded from the North, an unstoppable force who established their religion upon all they conquered. The Avestas, Gathas, Vedas and Babylonian epics all testify that their power was in the ones who led them.

The Bible says that the Nephilim tribes were 'great men of renown', a reference to their ability to destroy their enemies. The Egyptians, Greeks and others wrote about a land called Atlantis, a land which existed before the world's land mass moved apart. We know that continents moved and became what we have today, and we know that many smaller countries and islands like New Zealand, Hawaii and others are very young, so it isn't difficult to believe that other parts of the world sunk beneath the waves in the incredible upheaval that happened during the Great Flood.

The Bible's claim that eight people survived points us to an answer for the source of common beliefs. If Noah's sons re-populated the earth, moving North and South, this explains the oldest civilizations of the Egyptians and Aryans, and those who settled in the Mesopotamian basin. Their stories would all be the same, and as generations passed and people spread around the world, those stories would change slightly, especially if there were rulers with an agenda of their own.

According to the Bible, the Epic of Gilgamesh and the Book of Enoch, the giant races were the children of fallen angels, the ones who came from above, from the stars. They had one ruler over them, the one the Bible refers to as Satan, a fallen angel with a very specific agenda, namely, to keep humanity from having a meaningful relationship with the God he had rebelled against, and to stop the coming of the Messiah.

As early as Genesis chapter 3 we can read the very first prophecy given. This prophecy is given by the Creator Himself, predicting that a child would be born who would destroy Satan's authority over death. The prophecy also warned that Satan's kind would produce offspring, and in Genesis 6 we learn of these creatures who were born of 'gods' (fallen angels) and women - the very gods worshipped by every ancient culture and religion.

But there is one great mystery which stands above all others in human history - a book which not only records history, but foretells the future. The writings of the Aryans, the Sumerians, Babylonians, Hindus, Buddhists and Egyptians all record their past and present. They recall their victories and experiences of sacrifices; they recall the Great Ones who ruled over them, and later, the ideas which their gods taught them. The knowledge of the One God was never fully lost, but rather hidden beneath the demand to worship those who ruled them in their present situation. But one ancient book had a completely different outlook than all the rest - the Hebrew Bible.

The book of Genesis records human history and remains consistent with the history of other ancient texts and archaeology. The names of ancient cities are the same, and why would it not be so, for these people lived together and shared the same history, at least until they spread around the world. Genesis and Exodus, Deuteronomy and Numbers, the books of the Kings and Chronicles, all record the history of the Jews and their neighbors. Genesis introduces us to the figure of Abraham and his dealings with others whose names and cities appear in other writings.

The knowledge of the One God was not completely lost, for God had a plan to restore His relationship with fallen humanity. The Book of Exodus gives us a graphic account of Moses being used by God to go head-to-head with one of the most powerful civilizations in world history - the Egyptians. Their kings had adopted the same stance and claim as their legendary hybrid rulers - that they were gods themselves. The Egyptian records are consistent with the Bible's account, but for the student of religion, the lesson is not about one civilization conquering another as with the Aryans, but a spiritual battle of supernatural events between the Creator and the forces who bore the legacy of Satan's offspring.

The Jews were slaves; they had no means to fight for themselves. So the question to the person who denies the recorded events of supernatural origin must be, why would an Egyptian King who considered himself to be a god decide to release two million slaves? He wouldn't. The Egyptians had the most advanced technology of the time - chariots with swords protruding from the hubs of their wheels.

They drew their enemies onto the flat desert plains, raced their chariots around them causing great clouds of dust, and mowed them down while they struggled to see. There was no such battle with the Hebrew slaves, but still the Egyptians let them go, and somehow lost their greatest army led by Pharaoh himself. All of this is part of Jewish history and substantiated by archaeological evidence and hieroglyphics.

The Bible records the giants who had inhabited the land promised to the Jews - a concentrated effort to stop the prophecy being fulfilled, to stop the coming of the promised Messiah figure. The book of Leviticus is the revelation of God's character and rules for a functioning society at a time when slavery was a norm. Those laws, which the Bible claims came from God Himself, became, and still are, the basis of moral law almost globally.

But the great mystery was still to come. Up and until this point the Bible simply records one prophecy which was to be fulfilled in thousands of years, and many short-term ones which were fulfilled by the time the Hebrew tribes were established in their land.

Then God selected prophets and seers and began to pronounce what was going to come, or more importantly, *who* was going to come. Prophets were chosen by God, but there were counterfeits, mostly men who served the old gods, men who associated with the demon-inspired gods of the peoples who surrounded this small nation of Israel. God set a standard for the Hebrews to test whether or not their prophets were true or false. He gave His chosen prophets short-term prophecies. If these were not fulfilled to the letter the people executed the prophet and his family. In this way the true prophets lived to tell the future and record over 250 prophecies about the birth, life, death and resurrection of the Messiah whose name would be Emanuel.

There is only one ancient collection of literature which records the future. Its books are a great mystery to scholars and skeptics. The details concerning the life, death and resurrection of Jesus are so detailed, that from around the 17th century onwards, skeptics argued that these events must have been written after Jesus was born. Of course these skeptics had already decided that there was no such thing as the 'supernatural'.

This line of reasoning was difficult for Christian theologians to counter until a young Bedouin shepherd discovered large clay jars of ancient scrolls hidden in caves near the Dead Sea in Israel in the 1950s. Within the jars, many of the scrolls were disintegrating, having been written on papyrus and soft leather; however, there were also scrolls made of copper with the words stamped into the soft metal.

Carbon dating closed the mouths of the skeptics. Some of these scrolls could be dated centuries before the birth of Christ and the wording was exactly as in modern Bibles. All of those detailed prophecies about Christ had been given centuries before His birth; the question for the skeptic was 'how'? Where once skeptics had admitted the details in a bid to prove they must have been written after Jesus' birth, now they either ignored the facts or tried to re-interpret the prophecies to other events.

The Hebrew Bible is unique among all the ancient texts of world religions. It looks forward and predicts with absolute detail and accuracy events which could only be known by someone who can see the future completely. No other ancient writings contain prophecy.

And what's more, the Hebrew prophets often lived hundreds of years apart and each was given only certain aspects of Christ's life and death. King David, the man who established Jerusalem as his capital in the year 1000 BC, prophesied about the crucifixion of Jesus in incredible detail, at least 700 years before crucifixion was invented. Some 250 years later Isaiah told of Jesus' virgin birth and His life and sufferings in detail. Around 400BC another told of his birthplace, His flight to Egypt and other details. These men were never copying old stories; each was given specific prophecies.

What explanation can be given? For the skeptic, the answer is none. Statisticians calculate that the chances of just one of the prophecies about Jesus being fulfilled by chance are around one billion to one. Multiply that by 250 prophecies and you have a number which makes the skeptic look like a fool. So why are people so reluctant to believe?

The Bible would answer that question in another unique way, in a way that nearly all other ancient religions are silent about. Sin! The Aryans had no word for sin; they simply submitted to their god/warriors and destroyed their enemies. The Brahmins made 'Brahman' (God) subject to themselves, and eventually decided that they were gods, echoing the words of Satan in the Garden of Eden - 'you will be like God'.

Zoroaster wrote the Gathas, trying to get the people to conform to godly ways, but those that came after him used Soma, a powerful drug to communicate with demonic forces. They wrote the Avestas which brought the people back to obeying their possessed Shamans and the worship of demons.

Sin is a word that we don't like to hear, but a word used by God throughout the Hebrew Bible, and into the New Testament, by the One who fulfilled every prophecy about Himself - Jesus Christ. He was born where Micah said He would be; His parents took Him to Egypt to escape the wrath of Herod; He lived in Galilee and brought 'light to the Gentiles'; He had a forerunner in John the Baptist; He performed thousands of miracles and was crucified for claiming to be exactly who He was. But He rose from death - not reincarnated into some other body, but exactly as Isaiah said He would. All of the ancient prophecies which spoke of His earthly life and death were fulfilled.

But Satan wasn't content to be beaten by the resurrection of Christ. The Gnostics and Kabbalists tried to reinterpret the Hebrew Bible into hidden messages; they wrote false 'gospels' about the life of Jesus, giving hope to the skeptics who wanted His message of repentance and the Kingdom of God destroyed.

Then onto the scene came a man who used a similar intoxicant to Soma, a man who worshipped the same gods as the ancients - a man called Mohammed. He plagiarized the Hebrew Bible, replacing God's name with the name Allah. But he didn't simply change God's name; he denied the deity of Jesus Christ; he refused to comment on the prophecies, and wrote what his angelic educator told him. Allah and Jehovah, Mohammed and Christ have nothing in common; one is simply a counterfeit of the other - a desperate attempt by Satan to rally against the defeat he received at the cross of Christ.

And it would seem that Satan has few if any new or original ideas. His servants, Helena Blavatsky, Alice Bailey and the like, founded companies like the Lucifer Publishing Trust (1922) and studied ancient texts looking for similarities and ways to discredit the Bible. They found, as we have, that ancient religions had an incredible amount of ideas and philosophies in common, and why would they not?

They were inspired by 'gods' who had the same agenda - 'gods' who themselves had rebelled against their Creator and used their power to force, coerce and fool humanity into the same error. Blavatsky understood that the Bible was different. She, like the Kabbalists before her, had no option but to claim that its true message was hidden between the lines; that sin didn't exist.

The New Age movement is the ancient age in new clothes. Its emphasis is as old as rebellion itself, as old as the original sin - to promote the creature's rebellion against its Creator, to defame the very origins of our humanity. Blavatsky rightly identified the giant/gods of the past, however, she, like so many before her, believed their message that we are gods, apart from God. Human pride is a powerful motivator.

Today, millions practice forms of ancient religions in the hope of finding answers to their empty lives while avoiding that nasty word 'sin'. The world around us sinks deeper and deeper into problems which, without the recognition of sin, forgiveness and love, we will never find answers.

The Bible has not only prophesied the coming of Christ, but also His second coming. Scholars of prophecy, of which I am not, point out that Jesus' warnings about the Last Days, the time in which we are living, tell us that the events He predicted are happening on a day-to-day basis. Weather patterns are changing, signs are seen in the cosmos, economic foundations are disintegrating, and the world is increasingly seeing the need for global governance as a way to fix our greed and differences.

The Muslims await their own perverted version of the Messiah - a figure who will rule with extreme violence. Events in the Middle East in the past 70 years have fulfilled Last Days prophecies about the Nation of Israel - a nation which is central to understanding the Last Days.

The question for any person seeking the truth is where you will look. The history and mystery of religions should point in one direction. The tiny group of people to whom God chose to reveal Himself - the Nation of Israel - was like a little island of monotheism in a great ocean of demonic worship. From this nation came One who proved that He was not simply another teacher/prophet. He chose to allow Himself to be crucified as a sacrifice for sin, and then He did something which no other human being had ever done before or since, marking Him as absolutely unique in human history. He rose from death.

In the past 2000 years His words, and the teachings He left, have been misquoted, distorted and used to control millions, torture and execute innocents, dissected to fit His enemies religions, and also, to change and transform the lives of those who have really known Him.

God *is* knowable, for He has made Himself known in the person of Jesus Christ - a person that anyone with a hunger for truth can know. Meeting Him requires honesty and humility, for His hatred for lies and arrogance hasn't changed. The One who healed thousands, washed His disciple's feet, and took the punishment for sin by giving Himself as a final sacrifice for our sin on a Roman cross, will answer the cry of the humble seeker who asks in sincerity.

If this book has been part of your spiritual journey, then know that Christ stands at the end of the road waiting. The history of world religions is like a continuous battle to contain and destroy truth, replacing it with the age-old lie that we can be gods without God. The one human being who is God waits for us to come back to the Garden and give Him the authority to make us what He intends us to be - something far greater than any religion has dared to imagine or begun to accomplish, except that which He established.

Also by Steve Copland

Mary Magdalene: A Woman Who Loved

1st Century Trilogy - Book One

Throughout history there has been much written about Mary of Magdala, most of it legend and speculation, some of it derogatory. The Bible, however, gives us many clues as to the character, personality and contributions this first century woman made to the ministry of Christ and the early church. This book is, in many ways, a tribute to a woman whose life was dramatically changed by the one she came to love more than life itself.

Mary Magdalene was a woman whose life circumstances led her from demonic possession and prostitution to being the first witness of the greatest event in world history. In an attempt to reconstruct her life, this book demonstrates her struggle as she confronts the patriarchal traditions embedded in first century culture, the hypocritical practice of condemning only one gender in adultery, her transformation as she finds grace, freedom and real love in her encounter with Christ, and her being chosen as 'the apostle to the apostles'.

This novel takes the reader into the first century. It delves into the personal lives of lepers, cripples and the sight impaired; it goes on a journey from the battlefields of ancient Germania to Jerusalem with two Roman soldiers who end up initiated into the cult of Mithraism; it explores the fears, prejudices and arrogance of the religious rulers of Israel, and the ambitions of Judas Iscariot; it portrays the everyday struggles of first century people in an occupied land; it looks behind the scenes at a woman who is seduced into committing adultery and used to test Jesus, and brings them all together beneath the cross of Jesus Christ.

Simon and Simon: Passion and Power

1st Century Trilogy - Book Two

Simon and Simon is the second novel of the 1st century trilogy. It features two men born just a few miles apart whose lives are dramatically different, Simon Peter and Simon Magus. Simon Peter's life weaves through the story and is contrasted with Magus, the one known as 'Simon the Sorcerer'. The latter travels to Kashmir and studies the Rig Veda in search of individual power. He returns to Israel where he meets Simon Peter. Both end up in Rome: one levitates for Nero, the other is crucified.

Triarius is a Roman soldier married for only a few months and sent to the Northern frontier. His wife is pregnant when he leaves and believed to be carrying a son, if the witch was correct. He sends orders to dispose of the child if the hag is mistaken. His wife gives birth to a daughter, 'Triaria', and secretly raises the child while her husband is away, not knowing if he will return. He does, and discovers the child's existence, and…well that would be telling the story.

Running The Race

Every generation of Christians face challenges in 'running the race of faith'. Living for Christ in the 21st Century is no exception. The Apostle Paul warned that 'the time will come when men will not put up with sound doctrine. Instead, to suit their own desires, they will gather around them a great number of teachers to say what their itching ears want to hear'.

We are living in such times. We should not be surprised, for Jesus warned us there would be many false prophets in the Last Days before His return.

'Running the Race' challenges the extremes, throws light on the shadows, and illuminates the path which Christ has set before those who have trusted Him with their lives.

Slug: The Reluctant Butterfly

Slug wants to fly, but he doesn't want to die. Slug is a beautiful story about our reluctance to allow God to transform us into what He wants us to become. Slug learns through his mistakes that many will lead us down wrong paths, but obedience to our Creator brings complete joy and fulfillment. Grunt, a crow and central character in the story, discovers the pitfalls of peer pressure, the power of forgiveness, and eventual self acceptance in his new life. (Children ages 7-11)

Time for Truth: A Challenge to Skeptics

Time for truth challenges skeptics to take a fresh look at the supernatural qualities of the Bible. Issues such as the existence of God, creation/evolution, evil and suffering are discussed, and the reader is taken on a logical, scientific and inspiring walk through world history as a story of God's plan for humanity. This book has been used in various forms since 1985 when it was first written for a man dying of cancer. He refused to speak of God. He was an ardent atheist; however, he had a spiritual transformation just three days before he died and witnessed of his faith in Christ.

Perfection

Within the human soul a voice calls us to reach for perfection. In every area of our lives we demonstrate a desire to know, experience and create that which is perfect. The clothes we wear, the flowers we choose, religions we practice and love we seek, all testify to our instinct to reject that which we perceive as flawed, and strive for beauty, contentment and fulfillment. Is it possible for us to know and experience perfection? The answer is 'yes'.

Just Because: The Story of Salvation for Children

Just Because takes children on an exciting and inspirational journey through the Bible. It gives them an exciting bird's-eye-view of God's plan unfolding as He prepares the world for the coming of Jesus Christ. Throughout the story Satan is watching out for the child who will "crush his head," (Genesis 3) and he endeavors to stop God's plan from unfolding. The reader knows who that special child is, and the story especially opens up the insights that point to Jesus throughout the Old Testament. Each chapter takes about twenty minutes to read and ends with a short Biblical lesson. Children love it.

Contact details for conference, seminar and book enquiries.

http://www.stevecopland.com
copland56@yahoo.co.nz
Facebook: Steve Copland
New Life Church Kiev Ukraine

Steve Copland is a self-supported missionary serving the Lord in Ukraine since 2003. He lectures on Biblical Studies and Church History at the International Christian University and serves in the pastoral team at New Life evangelical church.

Made in the USA
Middletown, DE
23 March 2016